POOL POINTERS

WITH MEGAN RATNER

Photographs by Donna Bacchiochi

AVON BOOKS ◆ NEW YORK

Acknowledgments

Special thanks to my mother, Mary Stevens, my family, and my cats. I would also like to express my gratitude to Abel's Club, Ruby Alabama, Amsterdam Billiards, Belinda Bearden, The Billiard Club, *Billiards Digest,* Blatt Billiards, Victor Conte Sales, Ernie Costa, Raymond di Michino, Michael Eufemia, Bob Gesslein, Eric Kerchan, Bob Kerrick, V. Loria & Sons, Tony Meatball, George Mikula, Madeleine Morel, Mike Panozzo, Ken Smith, Roger Starr, Gloria Waslyn, Bob Worth, Myron Zownir, my professional collegues, and the Pool Detectives.

An extra special thanks for the photography of Donna Bacchiochi and Bacchiochi Photo services of Ridgefield, Connecticut. Also, thanks to Jack and Jill Billiards, Brewster, New York for the photo session space.

POOL POINTERS is an original publication of Avon Books. This work has never before appeared in book form.

AVON BOOKS, INC.
1350 Avenue of the Americas
New York, New York 10019

Copyright © 1992 by Billie Billing
Photographs by Donna Bacchiochi
Published by arrangement with the authors
Visit our website at **http://www.AvonBooks.com**
Library of Congress Catalog Card Number: 91-45485
ISBN: 0-380-76136-X

Library of Congress Cataloging in Publication Data:
Billing, Billie.
      Pool Pointers / by Billie Billing ; with Megan Ratner.
          p.   cm.
      1. Pool (Game)   I. Ratner, Megan. II. Title.
GV891.B55   1992   91-45485
794.7'3—dc20   CIP

First Avon Books Trade Printing: April 1992

CONTENTS

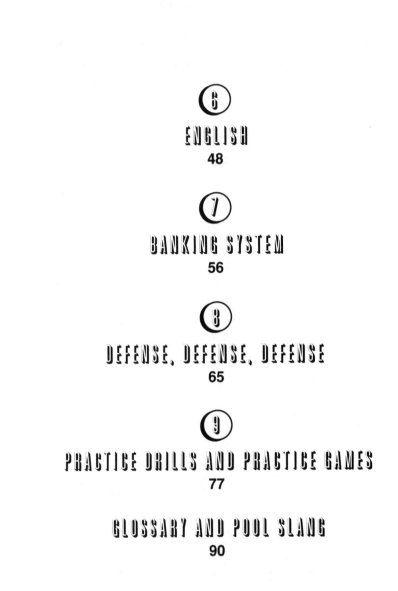

INTRODUCTION

Say the word "pool," and chances are people will see a dingy, smoky, windowless room. They'll imagine a hall peopled with shifty characters waiting to prey on them because they're not part of the hip pool crowd. Visions of *The Hustler*, or *The Color of Money*, pop into their heads. Like horse racing or dog fights, pool has a reputation for attracting cons ready to fleece the unsuspecting novice.

Too bad. Because, in fact, pool—real pool—has nothing to do with its down-and-dirty image. Well, not much, anyway. I mean, there are still the kinds of pool halls people associate with the term, and a few people who want to take advantage of new players, but far fewer than you would think. It's really hype. For a long time, many people kept away from the game, assuming you had to grow up with it to know how to play, and that's not true, either, as I plan to show you in this book.

Shooting pool is cool. In the twenty years I've been in the pool world, I've bumped up against lots of people who have had the wrong idea about the game. Even if they don't think all pool players are hustlers, they think playing the game is about extremes, all about tricks. But really hip pool, the kind I teach, is all about skill and technique. When you watch good players shoot, and I recommend that you do so frequently, it may look as though they're just hitting the balls which just happen to land in the pockets. In fact, they're combining art and science, using the physics of the game and their own creativity to play. As a woman, I'm well aware of the closed world pool can appear to be. Popular images like the aforementioned movies *The Hustler* and *The Color of Money* showed men, and then only certain men, playing the game. I was unwelcome at first, almost an invader. My passion for the game won out, and I managed to convince them that I was serious. The fact is, pool players are a lot like musicians. You have to show you're serious, but once you do, people are willing to show you some moves. And, contrary to what many people think, it's all about control, moderation, and coordination—not swagger.

Real pros are not cons. Professional pool players share a total dedication to the game. They have to be pool-crazy; the game demands years of daily practice if you want to compete, and very few financial rewards at all but the highest levels.

Over the past eleven years, I have taught thousands of people at every level, and of all ages. The lion's share of my clients are beginners, but I get a lot of people who consider themselves advanced while lacking a firm grasp of the fundamentals of the game. This book is addressed to both the beginner and the intermediate player. If you find yourself at a plateau, unable to get beyond one level of competence, I suggest that you start at the beginning of the book along with the novices, so that you can start from scratch to eliminate any bad habits you've developed.

Ultimately, my objective is not to give you hard and fast rules that you have to obey in order to play this game. I hope to teach you to think on your own, to become so familiar with the principles of good shooting that you can begin to manipulate them to your advantage. Watch any top player, and you'll see a tremendous level of creativity, of downright savvy about how the balls work together on the table.

I want to stress my ideas on defense. Defensive moves can lead to more creative, more rewarding play. It's one of the more exciting—and neglected—parts of the game, particularly for recreational players. It's essential if you plan to compete at any level. There's nothing quite like the feeling of wriggling out of a tough situation when your opponent thinks they've really got you stuck: it's simply glorious.

Even if you don't plan to buy your own equipment, I suggest you read through "The Essentials." You will be aware of what sets good equipment apart from bad and you can begin to pressure your local billiard parlor into providing decent house cue sticks, decent balls, and decent tables to play on.

Naturally, you have to know how to handle your equipment, and that's why "The Basics" is a crucial chapter. If you don't know how to place your hands and feet properly, you might as well be playing with a toothbrush. In addition to having less control over your game, you will actually get aches and pains if you stand incorrectly. By persisting in incorrect technique, your errors become ingrained and you can actually complicate them by compensating with more errors. Once you feel comfortable with all the principles discussed in this chapter, you can move on.

It may seem odd to you that I would precede my discussion of aim with "Caroms and Throws." The logic behind this choice is the structure of the book: I want you to become comfortable with each part of the game—the equipment, your stance, and moving around the table. Over the years, I have uncovered the pattern in which people can accept this information. Just as no teacher would introduce subtraction before addition, I feel that you can't really aim until you understand that the cue ball is your messenger: it can only be as effective as your technique allows. Now that you're familiar with the cue stick, "Caroms and Throws" will teach you about the most important element: the cue ball. Once you understand how the cue ball spins and how the carom line determines its path, you'll have the basis for good, straight shooting.

I've included "The Whiz Wheel System" for aiming; this is a useful tool even for very advanced players. The best part of this system is that it forces you to focus on the object ball and to stay down over the shot. Remembering to stay down over a shot is a problem shared by all beginners; people just want to pop up. But even if your aiming skills are solid but a little rusty, the whiz wheel will give you a method for correcting your aim and a shortcut to getting back into stroke.

The next step is to learn "Cue Ball Position Without English." If I haven't aimed straight with my cue stick, I know right away that I've missed the shot. I can't overemphasize the importance of staying level, making sure you're in a straight line. Once you've mastered these fundamentals, you can begin to move up and down on the cue ball using top or backspins to get position. Think of these suggestions as training wheels on a bicycle. Eventually you can dispense with them, but initially you need the combination of the whiz wheel's eight angles and familiarity with the center ball position to make aiming instinctive.

At this point, "English" comes into play. With your knowledge of aiming and position play, you've given yourself the tools to begin to move horizontally as well as vertically on the surface of the cue ball. Don't be surprised if you have to remind yourself of certain principles—keeping your cue stick straight, staying low over the shot—when you begin to use English; you'll have to make further adjustments.

At this point, you should feel very comfortable with your cue stick and with moving the balls around the table. It's time to look up—to the banks, that is. "Banking Systems" will really teach you about the table, and should help you to see it in three-dimensional rather than flat terms. Keep in mind that I can give you a thousand tips on where to hit the rail, but if you don't follow through in a straight line, you're in trouble. Good bankers have their fundamentals absolutely under control. Many beginners and especially intermediates complain that my system doesn't work for them, but I suggest you try working with these methods and adapt them to your style before you dismiss them out of hand. You will increase your use of banks, even if mine isn't the system you decide to adopt. In my own shooting, I find myself banking all the time using high, middle, low, or draw, rather than hitting the cue ball left or right. Using English to bank can get you into trouble; it's far less adaptable if the table is running long or short.

Finally, don't skip "Practice Drills and Practice Games." Pool players and musicians have a lot in common; both vocations demand time, devotion to the point of obsession, and practice. Think of the drills as scales. You can't improvise until you have all the notes down cold. Spending the first ten to fifteen minutes of every pool session on drills will not only warm you up for play, but your eye and stance will begin to develop without your even realizing it. Simply throwing balls out on the table and running them will teach you nothing and will actually encourage you to practice bad habits. With a drill, you're shooting the same shot over and over. Just be sure to limit the time you spend on these drills or you'll end up hating them.

Once the drill is over, begin to play and have a good time. A short practice game with your opponent will help both of you tighten your technique. It's very helpful to have someone critique your style and give you pointers. I play these games all the time with my students and I see improvement in their game—and my own.

The main objective of my teaching is to relax you and help you enjoy yourself. Pool has long been shrouded in a cloak of mystery with skills passed down haphazardly. My aim is to open the game up to everyone, to clue you in to what makes good shooting the best form of entertainment I know.

THE ESSENTIALS

An introduction to the billiard table, cue stick, and other accessories. Tips for choosing and caring for these tools of the trade.

Pool requires very little equipment, but even the novice player should know about tables and cues, and their accessories. Though I know that not all my readers can afford to buy a table, if you are at all serious you should invest in a cue stick.

Cues

There are various types of pool games: snooker, pool, and billiards. Although there are similarities in the equipment used in each, my comments about cues specifically refer to pool. Ultimately, it is personal choice which dictates the weight, length, and taper of your cue. However, I'd like to give you a few helpful hints. My thanks to Richard Black, one of the finest cuemakers on the planet earth, for some of the following information.

A standard cue is fifty seven inches long, but custom cues can be made from fifty six to sixty inches. I do not recommend a cue shorter, because it will limit your reach on the pool table. If a cue is more than sixty inches long it gets too "whippy" in front, causing you to lose control of the cue ball during play.

When shooting pool, all you are doing is making a six ounce, round, plastic object roll freely on a smooth, level surface in a four and one-half by nine foot area. At times, the cue ball has to contact one object ball (of equal weight and size) or perhaps open up clusters of object balls. You also want to maintain control over where that little white sphere is going. How much "weight" do you really need to accomplish that goal? You only need eighteen to twenty ounces. You can use twenty one to twenty two ounces for the break, but I don't advise that you play the entire game with it. It's not how heavy the cue stick is as much as how you stroke the cue ball that gives you power and control.

The problem with beginners is that they want to feel the heft of the cue stick in their hands. They gravitate to cues that are back-heavy. I promise you, the best-hitting cue is the one that is well-balanced, that feels like almost nothing in your hands. The balance point of a good cue is eighteen and one-half inches from the butt plate. However, break or jump cues could have a different balance point to fit the function of the cue. One-piece cues, usually the free sticks supplied by billiard parlors, tend to be heavier in the back and cannot be carried conveniently. A jointed cue (one that breaks into two parts) will be more expensive, but they are a worthwhile investment. Steer clear of cues that break into three or more pieces for regular play. The two main benefits of owning your own cue are that you get used to the feel of the cue's hit, and an enormous psychological lift, both of which will make you a better player.

The front of the shaft should be from twelve and one-half to thirteen and one-half millimeters. Again, it's personal comfort and your hand size that determine the width of your shaft. During play, you'll never need to follow through more than a foot. The taper of the shaft gradually gets wider from that point to the joint to give the shaft support.

For about 200 years, "points" were used on cues to help with their balance. Heavier woods were used in the back of the cue. The cut of the points also gave the cuemaker a larger surface area to apply the glue to keep the two parts together. There is also a pin that runs from the top of the butt through the wrap area. A second pin is placed at the end, inside the butt plate. Eventually, the points and the butt plate became decorative areas.

There are two main types of joints. The piloted joint and the "wood-to-wood." The piloted joint is made of stainless steel and sits at the top of the butt, along with a screw which protrudes one inch. The shaft end has a brass fitting that nestles inside the steel joint.

The flat joint is encased in plastic on the outside, with a stainless steel screw on the butt end. Inside, the wood is exposed: when the cue is put together, wood meets wood. To avoid stripping this screw, be sure to turn the shaft into the butt, rather than turning the butt into the shaft.

As Richard Black put it, "Ninety percent of the play of the cue comes out of the shaft, after you have a solid butt, and sixty percent of that play comes from the tip and the ferrule." The tip is what actually contacts the cue ball. It is made of pressed paper or leather, both of which are soft materials. If the tip were glued directly to the shaft, the wood would splinter over time; the tip is therefore glued to a piece of plastic called a ferrule. This absorbs the impact. You want both of these pieces to be flush with the shaft, so you will have a stream-lined aiming tool. The tip should be round, not flat. The contour should match the curvature of a nickel.

If there is an "overhang" of the tip, it should be cut down. Turn the cue upside down on a block of wood. Using a straight-edge razor with a handle, cut the excess tip off, slowly cutting and turning the cue until the tip is flush with the ferrule. You can also use a "shaper" for this job. This tool looks like a dome with a rough surface inside. Swivel the cue tip inside the dome until it cuts off the excess tip as described above, then take a piece of 400 sandpaper and carefully smooth out the sides of the tip. Wet your finger and run it around the sides of the tip; take a new bill—a five-dollar bill is fine, but if you want to impress your friends, go ahead and pull out the hundred—or put the cue tip under the rail and rub it back and forth. This will give a hard coating to the side of the tip, helping it to keep its shape a little bit longer. You should apply this coating every time you play.

Eventually, the tip will flatten. Use a file or a tool called a tapper (a pocket-size file) to re-shape the tip. Simply roll and press the tip against the tapper. It will mold the tip into the proper dome shape. The file pocks the tip of the cue, so that it will hold the chalk better—insurance against miscuing. (Most pool rooms will have all of this at the desk. However, if you want to be a player, I suggest you carry this material with you.)

A billiard parlor is the best place to test different cues, but if you're serious you'll soon want your own. Experiment by using rentable cues at billiard parlors rather than using the free one-piece sticks. Also, don't hesitate to ask pros and instructors in your local billiard parlor for advice. A reputable supplier is good too, though salespeople may not know enough to lead you to the proper cue. I've had my cues, Palomino and Rosita, for over ten years. They're nineteen and one-half-ounce, fifty seven-inch Palmer cue sticks. In 1990, Richard Black and Marad Shasha made me a gift of "Bridget," the cue I play with now. Richard designed her especially for me. On the butt plate, in sterling silver, are my initials and an impression of a camera, in tribute to my history as a pool photographer. Bridget plays like a dream. She's fifty seven inches long, but weighs only nineteen ounces. I noticed that a better-hitting cue lifted the development of my stroke. With less weight in my cue, I could easily execute finesse shots.

Caring for your cue is essential. My friend Gloria Walker learned to keep her cues close at hand the hard way. As she and her father packed for a tournament, Gloria quickly stuffed her cues into the trunk. Or so she thought. Not until they reached Chicago (a nine-hour drive) did Gloria and her father realize that the cues had ridden in the bumper! The cues always ride up front now.

If you nick the surface of the shaft, an easy and quick way to repair is take a piece of 600 sandpaper, and lightly rub the nick. Place a drop of water on the gouge. Let the cue lay flat, or lean it against the wall (in a corner to keep it from falling down) for about twenty minutes. If the nick is still visible, wet it again. Because wood swells, there's no need to use wood filler. Repeat the process until the nick sticks out a little from the shaft. You can then gently smooth it with a Scotch Brite scouring pad until it's flush with the rest of the shaft. Keep a piece of this material handy all the time to keep the surface of the shaft free of grime and grease. Unless you need to shape the cue tip, sandpaper is unnecessary.

Whenever your cue is not in use, lay it flat or stand it up in a supported position (in a corner, not just leaning against a wall). You can also store or carry your stick in a cue case. I recommend either a hard case or one that is well padded. There are many types. I think the ones with an accessory pouch and shoulder strap are the best.

When you're racking up, you want to put the cue across the table in front of you—otherwise the person breaking may jump the gun and send the balls right into your face. Leaning your cue against the table while you rack up just invites disaster. Inevitably, someone will trip over it, or it will slip, or you'll knock it over yourself.

Tables

Pocket billiards is usually played on four and one-half by nine foot tables. Whatever the exact measurement, the table is always twice as long as it is wide. The cushions (or rails as they are called) and surface of the table are covered with tightly woven wool cloth, generally green.

Though tables look much the same, they play differently. Your best bet is to get the feel of a table before you shoot a game. Lag the ball, sink a few balls into the pockets. Why wait until you're in a fix to find the table's idiosyncracies?

If you're considering acquiring a table for yourself, don't skimp. The table that only runs a few hundred dollars today is the white elephant of tomorrow. Without the ballast of solid construction—a slate bed, real, heavy wood, heavy-duty nuts and bolts, sturdy cushions—luck rather than skill will dominate the game and lead to frustration. You'll also need to find a place with enough space to move, about five feet all around the table. Though the going rate of $2,500 to $5,000 can seem astronomical, you'll get plenty of play from these tables.

Be sure to keep the table in good shape. The fabric should be brushed in the direction of the nap. Brushing against the nap can be equated with rubbing a cat's fur the wrong way. Don't do it. A special brush, sold in billiard supply stores (or available through mail order) will keep the ball return tracks clean.

A dust cover is also a good idea, especially if your table gets direct sunlight. You can use a sheet for this. Also, use a damp cloth to wipe any chalk smudges on the table and remember to wait until the table is bone dry before playing again.

Small rips or gashes may appear in the cloth as a result of miscuing. These can be repaired by placing billiard cloth repair tape—which you can find at a billiard supply store—under the tear. Wet the tape through the cloth and bring the sides of the rip together, pressing flat with your hand. If the cloth gets loose, try running an iron over it. Eventually, you will have to have it replaced by a table mechanic.

Though a good table can withstand the jostles and bumps of normal use, it's best to refrain from using it for storage or sitting.

I believe the Brunswick Gold Crown is the best table (and no, they don't pay me to endorse it). There are plenty of good enough tables, including other models made by Brunswick, but, as far as I'm concerned, the Gold Crown is the Cadillac of tables. Its unusual, sturdy internal structure makes it play truer than other tables. It's a combination of materials and craftsmanship.

Balls are made of baked plastic. Though they were mostly ivory until the late 1800s, very few players use ivory balls now. Composition (plastic) balls run fine, and are less likely to suffer cracks or get "out of round" and not run true.

THE BASICS

An introduction to stance and bridges. Using hands and feet properly is essential to shooting well. A good stroke relies on proper placement of the front and back hands. Finally, an argument for the much-maligned mechanical bridge.

I call this chapter "The Basics" because stance and bridges are the most important parts of your game. The best way to prove this is to watch pros play. You'll see that they bend, fold, and drape themselves over the table to make shots. I learned a lot about the game from watching, though I had help. I was lucky enough to run into a group of guys called the Pool Detectives.

Crazed with billiards, I attended the New Jersey State Championship in Elizabeth, New Jersey. I noticed a group of old men, real stereotype pool cronies, sitting up top of the bleachers. When I inquired, someone told me they were the Pool Detectives—they knew any and everything about pocket billiards. I sat near them the next day, struck up a friendship and learned an awful lot about rhythm, strategy and aiming. A few months later, I hitch-hiked from New York to Chicago to see the 1974 U.S. Open. Sure enough, I spotted the Detectives again, and planted myself within earshot. Though they themselves weren't great players, they were expert spectators and living proof of what a great game this is to watch. But I still think it's more fun to play and to do that you need to learn the essentials.

Though it may not be obvious to the casual observer, playing pool involves the whole body. A relaxed, strong stance will contribute to a smooth, gliding stroke, which will give you control over the cue stick. For this reason, this chapter is the most important in the book. If your body is off-kilter, your game will suffer. Like any other skill, personal style can develop once you get the basics down.

You'll soon see that the tripod image will come up again and again. Even though all your weight is on your two legs in the stance, it's important to keep this image of stability in your mind. Be sure to put all your weight on your legs, none on your front arm. (If you're shooting right-handed, your right hand will be on the butt of the cue, and your left leg will be in front of your right leg.) The idea is to keep your cue stick level. Remember that any elevation of the butt will cause you to "scoop" under the cue ball and probably make it jump off of the table. Part of keeping level is also staying down on the shot. A good way to stay down is to leave your bridge hand on the table until the ball goes in the pocket. Then you'll know you've completed the shot.

Think of your cue stick as a lever, your front hand as the fulcrum and your back hand as the weight. The weight at the back will give you power in the front. You have to direct this power very carefully. Elevate the back of the cue stick, and you will shoot down into the table. You will cause a backspin which deadens the ball's roll, or, as pool players say, kills it. You'll find that the speed will be all wrong also. Before you even worry about shooting, however, you want to be sure that you are addressing the ball properly, with the correct stance.

Stance

There are two types of stance: billiard and pool. Men will find it easy to distribute their weight more or less evenly between their legs, keeping both knees slightly bent. But, for women, this is a very difficult position. This is the classic billiard stance, but you can modify it for pool. The major difference is that you keep the rear leg straight, without locking the knee, while slightly bending the front leg. Learn to center your weight so that you don't lean on the table, or shift from foot to foot.

Your back foot should be directly under the cue stick with the foot at a three-quarter slant. Many people tend to turn their left front foot towards the cue or away from it—you want it to be parallel with the cue stick. Your back foot will be under the cue, your front foot will be about six inches left and parallel. Your body should be facing almost straight ahead.

How much or how little you bend is a matter of preference. Your chin should be about five inches from the cue, but you may get closer, especially if you learned to shoot young. (This is simply due to the fact that, as a kid, you had to stretch a lot more to hold the cue, which

Proper Stance

brought your face much closer to it. If you started off aiming that way, you've probably made subconscious adjustments as you've gotten bigger to keep the same aiming perspective.) People with eyeglasses will have to be a little higher to see over the frames of their glasses. Also, this height will change with the type of shot. Naturally, you'll need to be higher if you plan to shoot the length of the table than if you're very close to the object ball.

Once you're comfortable on your legs, look at your front hand. Your front arm should be straight. The straight arm positions your chin directly over the cue. Keep in mind that you are aiming the tip of your cue. This should be in line with the center of the cue ball; think about skewering *through* the cue ball and through the object ball rather than hitting and immediately jerking back the cue.

Placement of your back hand again depends on your height: for five-foot four-inch to five-foot nine-inch players with a standard fifty-seven-inch cue, the back hand should be about a foot from the butt of the cue. If your arms are especially long, move back about 6 inches; if they're short, move up 3 inches. The cue should feel balanced when held in both hands in a shooting position. To determine whether your back hand is properly placed, draw the cue stick back so that the tip of the cue comes to the edge of the point, where the cue rests on your bridge hand. This is the end of your stroke. As long as you are still level at this point, your rear hand is not too far back. If it were too far back, your arm would lift up when going back. This creates a "pump" rather than a level swing. When you "pump" the cue your forward motion causes a downward movement which can ruin your aim or change the deflection of the cue ball off the object ball. Ultimately, this leads to positioning problems for the player.

Think of your back arm as the pendulum on a clock. Keep your elbow down, no movement in your upper arm or shoulder. That back arm should travel smoothly. Cradle the cue, don't grip it. How you hold the cue is a matter of personal style, but it's a good idea to wrap the whole hand around the cue stick to begin with and to be sure that the back of your hand faces out, or just slightly turns up. A nice level cue should swing right through your shot. Remember the tripod image of your stance again, and make sure your head is directly over the cue at all times. Your back hand actually does all the work in shooting pool. Like the rudder which steers a boat. You must learn how to swing the cue back and forth in a straight line.

Proper Grip on Butt of Cue

The Six Basic Hand Bridges

Although you make bridges with your hands, there are other factors to consider as you learn them. If one eye has better vision than the other, be sure to compensate for that by positioning yourself for the best view. Your body shape will dictate how much you bend over the table, how you work out your stance. The most important idea is to keep your chin over the cue.

I talk about six different bridges, but the truth is, during actual play, you use elements of each one. Specific situations will call for a mixture of approaches, and as you practice all six of these bridges, you'll find that your fingers will stretch and consequently become more malleable on the table. As in other parts of this book, I stress the idea of options, different possibilities when you find yourself in a tight spot. Avoiding a particular bridge because you don't like it will spell trouble down the road. Similarly, at first you should try to emulate these bridges as exactly as you can. There will be plenty of time to cultivate an individual style as you play more.

I emphasize this, because bridges should be solid bases. Here again the image of the tripod applies. The cue stick should not have to fight your hand, it should be able to travel in a straight line. Again, remain level and remember not to give the hand on the table any weight. Also, bear in mind that the thumb is the most important finger in the bridge, because it acts as the chief support for the cue.

Open Bridge   This is a base for two other bridges (over-the-ball and open rail bridge). Begin by putting your hand flat on the table. Keep your fingers straight and raise your knuckles. You'll make a tent shape. Now, nestle your thumb next to your knuckle. Don't let the thumb come up too high. Be sure to keep the heel of your hand on the table, otherwise you'll disrupt the tripod. Now spread the other four fingers out and you'll have the necessary V shape. The V comes from the thumb; this makes the other four fingers appear to be part of the V. If you're worried about how high that V can be, remember that the cue ball is two and a quarter inches wide and you're aiming at the center of the ball. When the stick rests in the V shape it should be about one and one-eighth inches off the table. The tip of the cue should extend four to six inches beyond this V shape during your warm-up strokes. The distance your cue ball travels relates to the length of the follow-through on your last stroke. Since medium speed is what you

Open Bridge

should be concentrating on for now, you'll follow through from four to eight inches. Be sure your index finger does not face the cue ball directly, or your sight will be weak. You want the stick to move freely in the V. To assume proper position, roll your index finger slightly to the right. If you shoot left-handed, roll it to the left. The open bridge is easier for the beginner. More advanced players use it when they need to stretch to reach the cue ball.

Closed or Standard Bridge   This is the bridge you'll use for most of your shots. You'll have to turn your hand about a quarter of an inch more than in the open bridge, but don't turn it so much that it becomes uncomfortable. Swing your thumb so that it rests against the middle joint of your middle finger; the thumb is above that joint of that middle-finger joint. Make an "OK" sign and place the hand on the table; the heel of your hand is the base of the bridge. If you just lift your index finger away, you'll see the thumb and the fleshy part of the

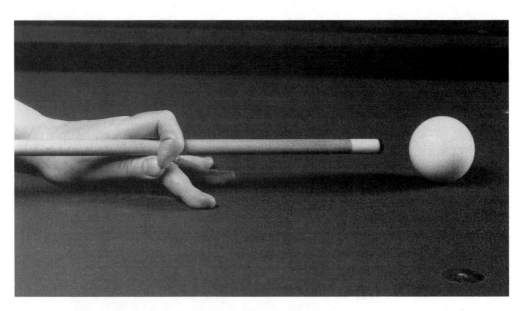

Closed or Standard Bridge

middle finger form a V. It's the same sight shape you saw in the open bridge.

This bridge will help keep the nose of the cue stick on your hand instead of lifting up in the air when you follow through. Resist the temptation to push down or squeeze the cue stick. This bridge needs a very light, gentle touch. And be sure to keep the index finger out of the way.

You should place your hand about four to six inches from the cue ball. This is where the sight should be. You can make adjustments if you put your hand closer or further back from the cue ball. For example, if you move your hand back, it will automatically put low on your stick.

Half-rail Bridge   This is an uncomfortable bridge, but one you'll need if the cue ball is too close to the rail to use a standard bridge. (This depends on the size of your hand, but generally the cue ball will be about 8 inches from the rail for a six-inch hand spread. If your hand is smaller or larger, the distance from the rail will change.) It takes some practice. You're nearly there if you make a standard bridge and put the heel of your hand on the rail. You'll notice that the tip of your cue is now above the center of the cue ball; however, you've got to

Half-rail Bridge

make an adjustment to bring the stick level again. To do this, drop your thumb so that it's lower than the joint on your middle finger. This means your index finger becomes part of making the bridge. The stick will fit nicely and neatly in that loop. You'll have to turn your hand another quarter of an inch to the right but be sure to remain comfortable, and as always, keep your chin right over the cue. You want to stretch out, so you can be a little further away from the table than on the table shots; feel free to crook your arm slightly if you want.

Open Rail Bridge   Though this bridge looks very fragile, it is a key bridge when the cue ball is frozen to, or up to 2 inches off the rail. This hand bridge looks somewhat like the open bridge, but you'll flatten the hand instead of making a "tent." Spread the thumb out so that the cue stick drops alongside the index finger. You also have the option of cocking the index finger at the knuckle to give you a larger guide. Since most tables have curved rails, by dropping the back of the hand off the table, the cue stick can stay level along the top, flat part of the rail, while the curve allows the back of the hand to go down and out of

Open Rail Bridge

the way. The way you stroke the ball is as important as your hand position. Because you are contacting the very top of the cue ball you could miscue. Short, deliberate warm-up strokes will help avoid this mishap. The natural tendency is to go back into a kind of wind-up and then shoot forward. Instead, you should concentrate on minimizing the backswing with this shot, putting the emphasis into the forward movement. Hit the ball dead center. Make sure your cue does not raise up off your bridge hand. It is your back hand which controls this shot.

V-Bridge This is a very easy bridge to learn. (Use this when the cue ball is 2 to 3 inches from the rail.) Lay your stick on the table. Line your thumb and middle finger up next to the stick. Put your index finger over to the other side of the stick. The rest of your fingers should be near the cloth of the rail, but do not curl them over the rail. Your fingers must always lie flat on the rail in these bridges.

Now your stick can ride right along your middle finger to the end of your thumb. The index finger comes to the other side of the cue stick

V-Bridge

which is completely flat against the hand. There should be no space between those three fingers. You'll notice that the stick will now ride smoothly on top of the nail and you can even stand a little further away from the table. Don't allow your back hand to drop or the tip of the cue will rise and probably cause a miscue. Also resist the urge to curl your fingers around the rail; this will give you too much room for movement and make the bridge unsteady.

Over-a-ball Bridge This bridge is simply a conversion of the open bridge. There are a couple of little tricks that are helpful for shooting over a ball. Fight the tendency to raise the palm and heel of your hand. Even though you're elevating your hand, you still need to maintain the V; the thumb is now next to the knuckle of the index finger. When you lift the heel of your hand, the thumb is useless, so keep it facing down, toward the table. This will give you the base. Your stance is almost straight up, with legs straight (but be careful not to lock the knees). Your back hand will be elevated, but you still keep the pendulum movement.

One mistake people often make is to keep their hand too far from the object ball—the closer your hand is, the more height you have. Balance your hand on the tips of the index and little fingers—they should be completely straight. The middle fingers curl up and back—keep them out of the way. There should be almost no pressure on your hand; be sure not to press down or you'll bend the fingers.

The best way to make this bridge is to place your hand first, then add the cue stick. You don't need the stick to set up, the V form of the thumb and knuckle will give you a natural aiming guide. This will stop you from fouling accidentally, or touching an object ball, or knocking into the cue ball. You'll tend to hit balls before you're ready if you put the cue stick and your hand on the table at the same time.

If you have very small hands, or need even more height you can balance on your middle and ring fingers. Though your hand will be slightly tilted, as long as it's straight, it's fine. Again, this bridge takes practice, but it's a great asset once you feel at home with it. You'll see some people spread out all their fingers around the object ball, which is fine if you have lots of room. But if you're surrounded by balls, learning this two-fingered bridge will get you out of tight spots even as a rank beginner.

Over-a-ball Bridge

The Mechanical Bridge   The dreaded mechanical bridge. Many people hate this piece of equipment, but really it is a useful and helpful tool. Once you learn to use it correctly, you won't mind it. Sometimes it can be a pain in the neck to reach down and get it in the midst of a game, but you'll see that the break in your rhythm can be worthwhile in terms of added flexibility.

Mechanical Bridge

There are three notches on the base of the bridge head. The two side notches should be the same size. You'll hardly ever use the slightly higher middle notch. Remember that the head of the bridge is a fulcrum: moving it closer or further away from the ball will adjust the height of where you hit your cue ball. The side notch should be directly at center ball. On the side of the bridge head, you'll see a higher notch. Use this to shoot over balls.

Your body should be square with the shot. Your hand is turned over—the back of your hand should face the ceiling. Your stroking arm will normally be down by your side, with the hand gripping the cue like a javelin, which will give you the pendulum swing from the elbow down. By putting your hand around the cue with the back facing the ceiling, you've just brought the same type swing up into the air. It's still the same movement from the elbow down. Be sure to keep your shoulder and the top of your arm still.

Wrap your thumb, middle, and index fingers around the cue. The bases of the little and ring fingers should be braced against the cue stick. This will make your elbow rise. Keep the elbow and the hand at the same level so that you are shooting with a nearly level cue stick.

Follow through, follow through, follow through. I can't emphasize enough how important this is. Your stroking hand should be right under or just in front of your chin to ensure that you follow through properly. Your stroke will become a poke if you keep the elbow down.

Now, bear in mind that all bridges are not the same. A really good mechanical bridge head design will allow you to swivel the butt of the bridge to one side. Unfortunately, many bridge heads are narrow and deep, which forces you to keep the handles of the bridge and cue stick together. Ideally, you want to get the handle of the bridge out of your way. For example, let's say you're drawing the cue ball, or hitting your break shot in straight pool; you have more control if you swivel the handle to the side. Hold the bridge handle to the left, assuming your cue is in your right hand, follow through on your stroke, and lift the bridge up. The cue stick will come, of course, right up too. But if you try to lift both simultaneously you'll miss your follow through.

Billie Bridge   Now, let me tell you about my innovation for short stretch shots. Since I've never seen any other pro use the bridge this way, I call this method the Billie Bridge.

You'll often see even top pros stretch for very important shots. They tend to miscue or miss the shot entirely, or not get the position for which they had hoped, because they refuse to use the mechanical bridge. To some extent, that's because using the mechanical bridge sets you off at a four-foot distance from the shot, and that can make a player insecure.

That's why I use the bridge as an extension of my hand. Since you're leaning over the table for a stretch shot, your body is balanced against the table, even if you're standing on only one foot. I put my hand about four to six inches from the bridge head and stretch my fingers out so that part of my body weight is on that hand. I then adjust to exactly where I want to hit the cue ball and shoot with my normal stroke. Just slide your normal back-hand position all the way to the end of the cue butt. By simply using the mechanical bridge as an extension of your hand, you'll have all the confidence you need for short stretch shots.

Billie Bridge

Now that you've read through the chapter you can spot any lingering problems by doing a quick review with this checklist:

1. Is your weight evenly distributed between both legs?
2. Is your front foot (left for right-handers) parallel to and 6 inches from the left of the cue stick, which is at 2 o'clock?
3. Is your back foot under the cue stick at about 2 o'clock? (10 o'clock for left-handers)
4. Is the arm of your bridge hand straight but relaxed, to help you to keep your head over the cue stick?
5. Is your hand bridge well-balanced and comfortable without pressing down?
6. Is your back hand cradling—not holding—the cue stick about a foot before the end of the butt?
7. Are your warm-up strokes confined to the first 6 inches of the stick?
8. Is your cue stick level?
9. Are you following through no more than 11 inches with a medium speed stroke?
10. Are you staying down on your shot?

CAROMS AND THROWS

Introducing two combinations important to the beginner, because they teach pocketing skills and improve confidence. Manipulation of speed and contact points are discussed.

Carom and throw shots will probably seem confusing at first, and you may even question my wisdom in introducing them before you've learned to aim. Believe me, there is a method here. Both these techniques teach about controlling the cue ball, the ultimate key to shooting a good game. Good play requires that the cue ball be set up for an easy next shot. In order to place your cue ball properly, you must be able to visualize the angle at which the cue ball deflects off the contact point of the object ball it has struck. You also need to know how striking the cue ball left or right of center will influence the path of the cue ball and/or object ball. Caroms start you thinking about the lines of deflection and throw shots give you a taste of how spin affects an object ball. Caroms and throws are easier shots for beginners to make because there's a bigger contact area for pocketing the combo than if you are shooting a single ball. They can be a great help to beginners who are still struggling with their hand bridges and back hand. Ultimately, they can spell the difference between adequate and inspired play.

But you have to know what to look for before you can begin to use the techniques properly. The first step is to recognize the four types of shots:

Combination   Two object balls and the cue ball. The space between the two object balls is wider than one-eighth of an inch, and your goal is to shoot one object ball into the other in order to to pocket it. Although there may be more balls in the cluster, your focus will be on the two object balls (Diagram 1.1).

Throw shot   Two object balls which are "frozen" or touching. If the balls are touching, or less than one-eighth of an inch apart, you shoot one ball into the other with an off-center contact point. This works best when they are frozen (Diagram 1.2).

Carom   Two or more object balls which are frozen or less than one-eighth of an inch apart. You shoot one object ball off of another object ball. Rather than shooting one ball into another (as in combination above), you use the second object ball to jettison, or "squeeze," the first ball into the pocket (Diagram 1.3).

Kiss shot   Caroming one ball off another when the object balls are more than one-eighth of an inch apart (Diagram 1.4).

Each of these shots requires an understanding of the cue ball. Earlier, I called the cue stick the most important piece of equipment. The cue ball is the extension of the stick. Think of it as flexible, fluid, alive. Using the dead weight of the object balls, you will learn to control the path of the cue ball, and keep a run going.

Caroms

Recognizing and using opportunities to make carom shots is crucial to your game. Begin by looking at the point where the two object balls meet (Diagram 1.3). Imagine a straight line, like a piece of fishing wire, that extends directly into the pocket from this meeting point. Think of this as part of a right angle. Now look at the pocket to make sure there's enough room for the ball to carom into it without hitting the rail. For example, if the line leads directly to the center of the pocket, you can make the shot with either object ball. If the line goes to the left of the pocket, you'll have plenty of room to pocket the ball on the right, but the left-hand ball will no longer fit into the pocket.

When setting up a carom shot, how do you figure out where to hit the cue ball to make the first object ball carom off of the second object ball and go into the pocket? Let's say you have (Diagram 1.3) Ball A,

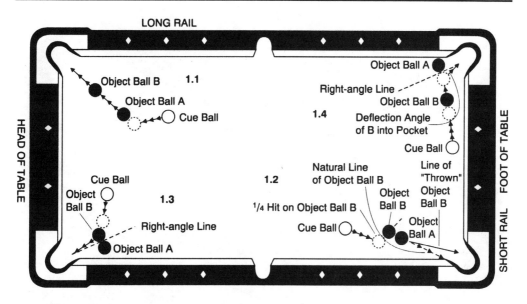

Diagram I, Combination, Throw, Carom, Kiss

1.1   Combination

Cue ball moves object ball A, which in turn hits object ball B, knocking B into the pocket.

1.2   Throw

Cue ball strikes object ball A on the right side, sending it to the left. Even though object ball B's natural line would take it into the rail, object ball A will modify that line, throwing B toward the pocket.

1.3   Carom

Cue ball strikes object ball B, which "squeezes" off of A along a right-angle line and into the pocket.

1.4   Kiss

Object ball B contacts A, and B deflects into the pocket along the right-angle line.

Ball B, and the cue ball. If A is to the left of B, and the cue ball is traveling to the right side of B, you'll squeeze B against A, forcing B to pop out and shoot along the right angle line, straight into the pocket. You must hit the cue ball in the center with medium speed, but you have six different contact points (Diagram 2.1) in an area of about one-half inch on the object ball. Hitting the cue ball too hard will push the two object balls that make up the carom shot to one side, causing you to miss. Hitting too slowly may cause the object ball to meander backwards. Practice setting up the shot until you've got a feel for the speed.

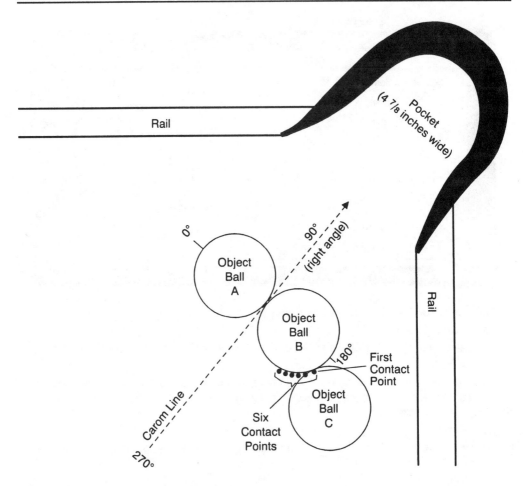

A = The object ball you are caroming, or "bouncing" off of.
B = The object ball being pocketed.
C = The "controlling" ball. Can be the cue ball, or another object ball.

Diagram 2, Carom Contact Points and Angles

2.1   Carom Contact Points

In order to create the "squeeze" necessary for a carom shot, the controlling ball (usually the cue ball) has to hit the ball that is to be pocketed within a certain area. That area on the object ball is about an inch wide. To make it easier to visualize, think of that area as containing six possible points of contact. Even though, theoretically, there are an infinite number of points within that one-inch space the cue ball's point of contact occupies a large enough area on the cue ball that—by moving the cue ball from point to point within that space—the number breaks down to six.

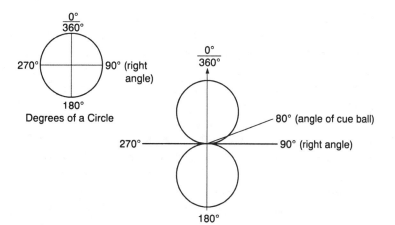

Degrees of a Circle

2.2   Carom Angles

It is easy to visualize the angles of a carom shot if you think of the two object balls as being in the middle of a circle. The 90-degree point of the circle is the line that the object ball which you intend to pocket will follow when the cue ball squeezes it off of the other object ball. The object ball that is causing the squeeze will be pushed out along the 360-degree line, and the cue ball will move along the 80-degree line. By modifying the speed of the shot and the cue ball's contact point on the object ball to be pocketed, you can control the cue ball to play position.

Remember that the object ball between the cue ball and the third ball is the most important, because it must contact the second object ball (ball B, in my example) at one of the six contact points to set up a squeeze play. When you have more than two object balls, it's very important where that third ball contacts ball B, because the third ball could obstruct the path of B once the balls start moving.

Carom shots are also a type of pack shot. That is, a shot where you target one ball in a cluster for pocketing. If there's a cluster of balls after the break in straight pool or 8-ball, it's very important for you to be aware of balls that are touching or less than one-eighth of an inch apart. Draw an imaginary line from where they meet to the nearest pocket. If you have trouble visualizing this, imagine there's a curtain between the two balls. Now extend the curtain to the pocket. That's the right angle line. If you see two balls at the end of the pack, and there's a parallel line where they meet that goes to the pocket, check to see if the object ball you plan to pocket has other balls behind it. If it does, you can make the shot and use the weight of the other object balls as a ballast to "guide" the object ball into the pocket. In fact you can hit the ball harder than if it were a simple squeeze play. If you've got an extra ball between the cue ball and the carom shot with no weight to help you behind the object ball, you'll need to hit the cue ball at a slower speed. If you know how to use the weight and movement of the cluster to your advantage, you'll not only pocket a ball, but break up the pack. If you're not careful, you'll actually throw the shot off, and the ball won't go in the pocket.

You'll notice I keep mentioning those six contact points. The cue ball will travel off of an 80 degree line from where the cue ball meets the object ball. It's the same principle as the carom shot, only your cue ball is now part of the shot rather than just the instigator, since you're trying to "get position" for your next shot (Diagram 3). Any time your cue ball becomes more active, speed becomes more important. You'll always get a little less than a right angle off of the contact line where the cue ball and the object ball meet, assuming medium speed and a

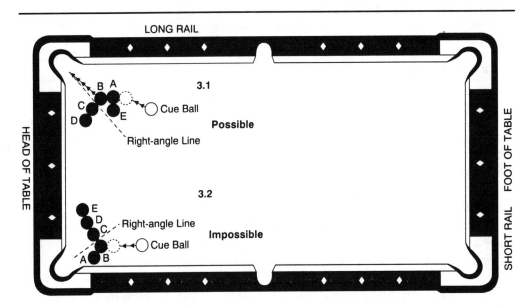

Diagram 3, Cluster Carom

3.1 Possible: Cue ball strikes A, which becomes the controlling ball and squeezes B off of C along the right-angle line. Balls D and E do not figure into the equation, although you can hit the cue ball harder than normal if you wish, because D's added weight behind C will act as a ballast and keep the shot from getting out of line.

3.2 Impossible: This cluster carom won't work, because ball A will bounce off of the rail, and interfere with B.

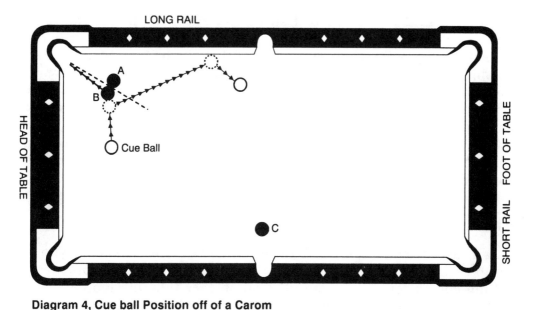

LONG RAIL

HEAD OF TABLE

FOOT OF TABLE

SHORT RAIL

A

B

Cue Ball

C

Diagram 4, Cue ball Position off of a Carom

By learning the angle at which the cue ball will deflect off of an object ball, you can obtain position on your next shot. In the diagram, the cue ball will come off of B—which will go into the corner pocket—and come off of the rail uptable for position on ball C.

center-ball hit. The cue ball will travel off of that parallel line. Speed and where you hit the cue ball will affect the shot. Having six contact points to choose from gives you more flexibility about where you hit the object ball for positioning purposes. By making the cue ball's angle of impact on an object ball slightly "thinner" or "fuller," you change the angle and speed at which it moves when it comes off of the object ball. Learning to control these factors will make it easier for you to put the cue ball in line for the next shot.

One good example of this was a shot I saw pro Allen Hopkins make a few years ago. Playing 9-ball, he found himself in a tight spot. He was shooting the four, which was tied up with the six ball about a diamond and a half below the left top corner pocket. The cue ball was in the lower right hand portion of the table. Hopkins had to figure a way to pocket a ball, and gain position on the five ball, which was frozen to the top rail, to the right of the four and six. A close view of the balls showed that the four would not go in off the natural carom angle. Rather than trying to shoot a carom with a slow cue ball—remember, I mentioned earlier that cue ball speed can affect the line of the object ball—Hopkins decided to play the six ball in the opposite top corner pocket. He figured out the carom line of the four ball, and found that a combination with moderate speed would pocket the six and leave the four hanging near the corner pocket. This would also allow him to get position on the five. Hopkins made the shot and ran the remainder of the rack.

This is the only physics you'll need to know, but you've got to learn to spot these shots and use the other balls on the table in concert with the cue ball.

Throw Shots

As I mentioned, throw shots occur when two object balls are frozen or up to an eighth of an inch apart. Remember that these shots involve hitting one object ball *into* another one rather than *off* another object ball. They require you to contact the object ball closest to you (B) off-center with the cue ball in order to shift the second ball (A) in the desired direction. The amount of shift you need determines how much off-center and at what speed you hit the cue ball. When shooting a combination (that is, two balls which have more than an eighth of an inch space) to the left pocket, you strike B on the left to move it right and A will also move left (Diagram 1.2). This goes against logic, and you need to practice the shot to get a feel for how it happens. Normally, you would expect a ball struck on the left side, as B is striking A, to move to the right. But, as long as the balls are touching or less than an eighth of an inch apart, a proper touch will "throw" A to the left along with B.

The base rule of the shot is that if the cue ball contacts the quarter point of object ball B with a medium speed, center-ball hit, object ball A will shift over *one inch* for every *foot* it travels forward. Keep your cue level.

You can change the amount of shift you want on the throw shot by contacting more or less of B to correspond with where the shot lies on the table. Divisible fractions other than the quarter-ball hit are one-eighth, one-third and one-sixth. Be sure you measure the required shift separately from the distance to the pocket. Unlike caroms, hitting the cue ball above or below center will not affect the shot, but avoid using left or right English.

Another influential factor is the speed you use on the cue ball. The slower you hit the ball the more throw (or shift) you'll get. Hit the ball harder and you'll diminish the throw. The slower moving object ball simply has more time to shift over, sometimes even more than one inch per foot. Be sure to factor in the speed of your shot when you plan a throw shot.

This may seem confusing, but once you try some of these shots you'll see that they really open up your game. The most important concept is that the cue ball is crucial to your strategy. Think of it as malleable, changeable, alive among the dead object balls. Hitting the cue ball to the right or left of center will throw the object ball more, so stick with center ball until you're fairly proficient before trying English. Hit the ball softly, you'll get more throw, hit it harder and you'll get less. The better you know your cue ball, the more you can use positioning techniques like English, and the better you'll understand aim.

THE WHIZ WHEEL SYSTEM

The Whiz Wheel blends two popular systems—the ghost ball and mathematical formulas for aim. I like it because it gives a real target to shoot at and makes the player concentrate on looking straight down the cue stick. The beauty of this system is that it strengthens your pocketing ability by improving your eye and your stroke.

As you read through my instructions, you may find yourself forgetting one of the fundamentals of pool, the fact that we're playing with round objects. Because there are two spheres, point of aim and point of contact are in two different locations. You are, in fact, aiming the center of the cue ball at the object ball, allowing of course for the fact that these are spherical objects rather than round discs.

You'd be amazed how people can forget this fact as they try to take aim. The Whiz Wheel will show you that there are only nine shots on a pool table; straight on, and eight angles. It also helps to orient you, to give you a sense of where the center of your cue ball is.

The Whiz Wheel also helps with a common and nagging problem. It will help to get your cue stick going in a level, straight line. If you stick with medium speed shots, you'll soon find your stroke will develop as well.

Even if your level of play is intermediate, it's easy to get out of stroke. The Whiz Wheel will give you a system to gauge against. It is also a good back-up if you find yourself in a tense, stressful game and you're not shooting at your best. Going back to the formulas to aim your shots will narrow your mind to the task at hand and dissipate the worry and stress. Using the mathematical formulas, you can begin to see whether you're missing because you're misjudging the angle or not following through in a straight line, to name just two examples.

Many instructors like a "ghost ball" aiming system. (Keep in mind that this will only work on a standard table; oversize cue balls on bar tables throw the system off.) Find a contact point by pointing your cue stick at the object ball and then toward the pocket. That's your "ghost ball" contact point. Try to imagine one and one-eighth inches from that point and that's where the center of your cue ball is going to sit at the point of contact with the object ball. With the Whiz Wheel, you can look at the cue ball and see that it lines up with a fraction of the object ball's surface at a particular angle. This will give you the contact point and the aiming point. The straight-on shot is the only one in which both points are the same.

Now, figuring out one and one-eighth inches is not easy for anybody, so I'm afraid I'm going to suggest that you do something you probably haven't done since grade school: memorize. Just as you once had to commit the alphabet to memory to learn how to read, you will make your life much easier if you memorize the eight angles. That way, you'll be able to recognize them when they come up and you'll start to notice that you can see the fraction when you continue from the cue ball to the object ball along the line. The only way to get to this level, however, is to bring the Whiz Wheel to the table with you and practice with it.

The angles to look for are: straight on, one-eighth of a ball off the center of the object ball, quarter of the ball, the edge (half ball), plus-one- and-one-half cue tips from the ball, two, three, and four tips. Plus-one starts where the half ball ends. At half tip, your cue stick is half on, half off the cue ball, so when you move it over to shoot plus-one, you're actually one and a half tips from the edge of the ball.

With the Wheel on the table, simply slip the front notch of the Wheel under the object ball, take the bold arrow in the center and point it towards the pocket. You then place your cue ball along one of those lines—one-eighth, quarter, whichever you choose to practice. If the cue ball is between two lines, you can probably shoot in either direction. When you're more familiar with the system, you'll start to see when you're between two angles; you'll know the angles so well that you'll see when you need a little more or less to pocket the ball.

The main idea of this system is to give you more confidence in your shooting. If you're shooting well, there's no problem, but if you start missing, you'll have to start naming the angles. Contrary as it may seem, that kind of concentration will actually jolt your instincts back, and you'll start relying on them rather than thinking about specific fractions.

If you use the system without the Wheel, try marking the angles with small wet spots on the felt (I generally wet my finger), and placing the balls on those spots. It's a good way to set up a shot over and over again, and you can't see anything when it dries. It's much better than just putting the cue ball down anywhere and eyeballing angles. Unless you mark the shot, you won't be assured of practicing the same shot again and again.

Aside from getting to know the nine shots, you'll also improve your knowledge of the table using this system. The topography of the table will begin to give you clues about shots. You'll start to see that shots in certain parts of the table are always one-fourth or half-ball shots.

Also, don't forget the spot shot (Diagram 4). Put an object ball on the foot spot and, as you face down-table, place your cue ball a ball's width from the rail at the level of the first diamond (base line). Let's say you're going to cut into the left corner pocket. That's exactly a half-ball shot, what some pros call a one-and-one-eighth shot. You aim your cue stick at the edge of the object ball and follow through at medium speed. You can hit the ball harder or softer, but practicing at medium speed will give you more control and help you to hit straight through and in a smooth, level line.

As you can see, the Whiz Wheel is useful and fairly self-explanatory. The following checklist should help you to remember the main characteristics:

1. You may have to memorize the angles on the Wheel at first, but eventually they will become instinctual.
2. The Wheel gives you a practical device you can use when you are doing drills.
3. The carom angle of the cue ball becomes more apparent, because the system makes you focus on the contact point in order to calculate the shot.
4. By understanding where "point of aim" is with center ball, you can make an adjustment for any English you might apply.
5. Concentrating on a concrete mathematical formula will help you relax yourself during tense game situations.

Whiz Wheel System

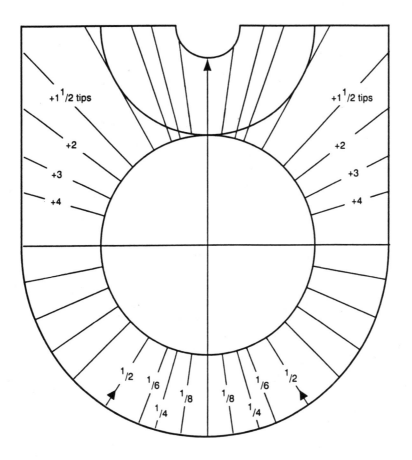

CUE BALL POSITION WITHOUT ENGLISH

Many people assume that English is crucial to cue ball positioning. Not so. Hitting the cue ball high, middle, low, or with draw is a much more accurate and effective method for most shots.

Sometimes I watch people trying to teach their friends to shoot pool, and they'll talk about spin, left spin, right spin. It always baffles me that people think you always have to put spin, or English, on a ball. (Although technically hitting the ball high or low is also English, it generally refers to left or right.)

When I first developed my interest in pocket billiards, I read Willie Mosconi's book. I remember my surprise at his statement that he shot at center ball seventy-five percent of the time. How could he possibly? I figured he must have an enormous knowledge of pattern play or such total control of the speed of his shots that he didn't have to bother with English much. When I played, I just couldn't manage to get position on the ball without going right or left of center.

At that point, I had no idea about how much it was possible to manipulate the carom line off of the object ball by simply hitting the cue ball high or low. It wasn't until about five years later that it dawned on me that I could change the angle off of the object ball by simply hitting higher or lower on the cue ball (Diagram 5).

The cue ball will come off of the object ball at an angle of 80-85 degrees. In other words, it will be just short of a right angle. This line that the cue ball follows is called the "carom line." (See Chapter 3 for a

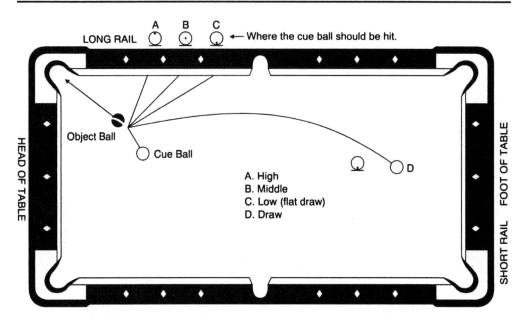

Diagram 5, Cue ball Positioning Without Sidespin

A medium speed, center-ball hit would cause the cue ball in this case to come off of the object ball at almost exactly a 90-degree angle (B). By hitting the cue ball with high English, we make the deflection angle smaller. Low English—also called flat draw—will widen the angle. Draw will greatly increase the angle, causing the cue ball to curve slightly as it comes uptable.

detailed discussion.) First, look at the ball you intend to pocket. Now figure out where your cue ball will have to contact it. (You will probably want to use your cue initially, though eventually you can just eyeball it.) That contact point is the base of your angle. You can then hit the cue ball in the center at medium speed. Don't forget that changing the speed of your shot will change the angle slightly. You'd have to hit the cue ball pretty slowly to knock it off of the right angle, but if you hit it hard, the speed is liable to force the cue ball off in a wider angle of deflection.

A good rule of thumb is to visualize high as two cue tips above center, low as two tips below. (This is a bit exaggerated. One or one-and-a-half cue tips will usually suffice. Try it with two cue tips' distance to get the feel.) If you hit high, your cue ball stays with the object ball a little longer. Even though the cue ball will appear to go off the right angle, in fact the angle has shifted. It's the same idea as when you change speed. You're actually shortening the point of contact on the rail. If you hit the ball low, be sure to keep your cue level otherwise you'll make a draw shot rather than hitting low. This is also known as flat draw; you should feel as though you're hitting dead-center on the ball and that your back hand is not too loose. The difference between low English to draw the ball and low English to merely stop or slow it down will be easier to visualize if you substitute a striped ball for the cue ball. With a striped ball, you can see the effect that different strokes have on the spin. If you can get a clear picture in your mind of what the cue ball is doing when you hit it, you'll be able to control it better. Remember that a real draw shot will feel as though you're almost throwing the cue at the ball. You should feel more control in this version of the shot.

What's actually happening here is that you're giving the cue ball an underspin. This will give it more traction on the cloth, and will widen the angle a little. Again, substituting a striped ball for the cue ball will help you visualize this. Good players move all over the table this way.

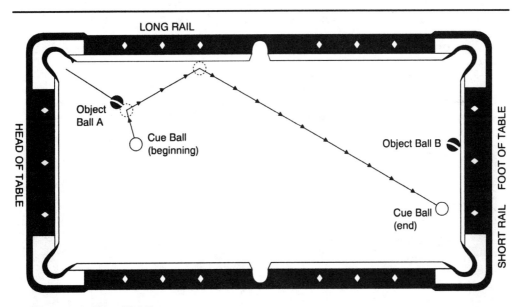

Diagram 6, More Flat Draw

The first time I show this shot to my students, they invariably say that sidespin would get the cue ball into position for object ball B. While that might work, it would be simpler to put flat draw on the cue ball, which would widen the angle of deflection and bring the cue ball uptable.

By widening the angle of rail contact they widen the angle of deflection off the rail. Many people are convinced that you have to use English to do this, but simply widening the angle will motor you all over the table (Diagram 6).

This is not to say that there aren't a few shots on the table where you have to hit the cue ball right or left of center in order to pocket it, but I would say 98 percent of the time you don't need English to pocket balls. You do need to use it to play position.

The following is a practice game I teach my students. It will show you more about combinations and how to manipulate the angle of deflection of one ball off of another. In this game, you're shooting the object ball off of—or into—the cue ball.

Reverse Billiards

The rules of Reverse Billiards are relatively simple: You are shooting object balls into or off the cue ball. Hence, you are "reversing," or turning the game of pool around. It's more like billiards than pool.

You may make four different basic shots in Reverse Billiards:

1. An object ball off of the cue ball into the pocket (Diagram 7.1).

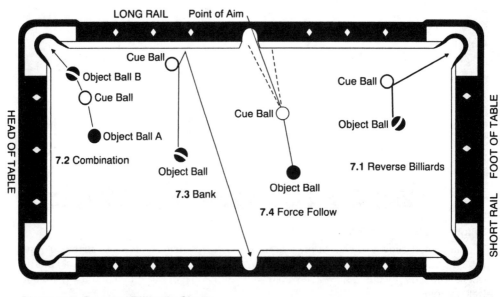

Diagram 7, Reverse Billiards Shots

2. An object ball into the cue ball into one or more object balls (Diagram 7.2).

3. An object ball into the cue ball, then into a rail or rails, banking that object ball into the pocket (Diagram 7.3).

4. A force follow shot. Line the cue ball and object ball straight into the rail, then line the cue ball up with the pocket. Halve the distance between these two lines to get your point of aim. Aim at the cue ball so that your object ball is lined up with that half-way mark. Hit it with a heavy follow stroke. It's not necessarily a hard hit as much as plenty of follow through that makes this shot successful (Diagram 7.4).

Two players compete for the eight points that win the game. You must call your pocket in this game. If the ball drops into the wrong pocket or you sink any extra balls, they come out and go to the foot spot, or as close as possible down the center line. These extra balls

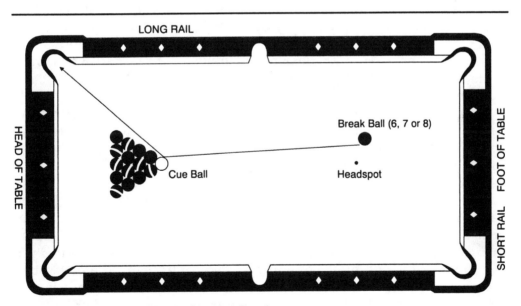

Diagram 8, Reverse Billiards Opening Break

Rack up fourteen object balls with the cue ball on the foot spot. Place an object ball approximately halfway between the center and first diamonds, just beyond the head string. If you're right-handed, the ball should be on the right side of the table. Shoot the object ball, aiming to contact the lower-right edge of the cue ball with a high, hard stroke. The break ball will go into the upper right-hand pocket, and you'll open up the rack.

come up after your turn is over, unless all the other object balls are already off the table and you still need one to win.

To start (Diagram 8), rack with the cue ball on the foot spot, the other balls behind, just as though you were racking for 8-ball. (This is known as a full rack.) Put the break ball about three to six inches to the left or right of the head spot. Use the darker object balls (six, seven, or eight) when shooting the opening break shot. The chalk might smudge the ball and is less visible on the darker surface. Calculate the carom to shoot that ball off of the cue ball and into a corner pocket at a hard speed to bust the balls open (just like a break, but it's as if you were scratching on the break). This is the best way to break, since you must always call your shots. Any additional balls that go in come back up on the table after your turn is over, and are not counted as points.

If you pocket the cue ball (pocket scratch) it goes to the head spot at the top of the table. If an object ball was pocketed on a scratch, it comes back up on the foot spot, and you owe a ball for scratching, which spots up as well. The next shooter must play off the cue ball from that spot. If the head spot is occupied, you may place the cue ball in the center of the table. If both spots are taken, put the cue ball as close to the head spot as possible. (I have never played when both spots were occupied. I'll leave it to readers who have this experience to write in and tell me how they coped.)

You commit a foul if you don't hit the cue ball or if you don't hit the cue ball first (table scratch). You have to return a ball to the table, or, if you haven't scored, forfeit your first point and the first ball you've legally sunk comes back on the table.

Even if you've contacted the cue ball first, but you don't manage to pocket anything, you must hit a rail after making contact with the cue ball to avoid committing a foul. These "table scratches" give your opponent the option of leaving the cue ball where it is, or spotting it up as though it were a pocket scratch. If another object ball is in your path, you must call which ball will go in, and you must sink the called ball without touching or caroming off of the other object ball. That is, the object ball must go in "clean" unless you call it off of the other ball.

As I explained in far more detail in Chapter Three, caroms consist of medium speed shots in which the cue ball comes off the object ball at almost a right angle from the contact point. If you hit the cue ball a tip above center, you will shorten the angle of deflection of the cue ball. The topspin on the cue ball will cause it to stay with an object ball

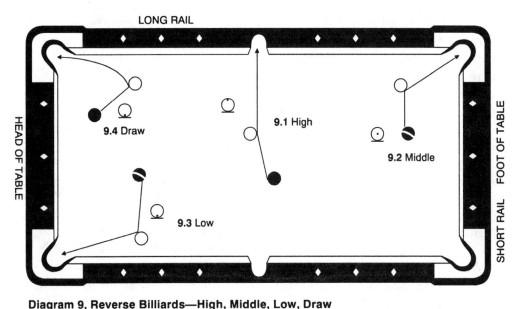

Diagram 9, Reverse Billiards—High, Middle, Low, Draw

Points can be made by caroming object balls off of the cue ball. Choose a high (9.1), middle (9.2), low (9.3) or draw (9.4) hit, depending on which best suits the angle to the pocket.

longer. When the cue ball hits the rail, it will hit below the original angle off of the object ball.

Hit your cue ball low, and your angle of deflection widens off of the object ball. Technically, hitting the ball low is draw, but my definition is more specific. Hitting the shot with draw means elevating the back of the cue a bit more. Loosen up your back hand. You should feel as though you're almost throwing the cue stick at the cue ball. Actually, you're using the weight of the stick to cause the backspin. You thus apply a subtlely different touch—finesse—to the shot which makes the cue ball come back in an exaggerated way, called "draw" (Diagram 9).

If you hit the cue ball below center with a follow through, it's a flat draw. Rather than boomeranging the cue ball back directly, this shot widens the angle of the cue ball. Thus, you're still drawing the ball, but it's not getting as much draw as when you put in the finesse and elevate the back of the cue stick. Make sure you keep the cue level and hit the cue ball lower. By lowering your front bridge hand, you can contact the cue ball below center and maintain a level cue stick. (One note here: many beginning players have trouble understanding and applying the idea of follow through. When you aim at the cue ball, imagine your cue stick skewering the ball. You want to feel as though you're shooting *through* the ball.)

In this game, you will hit the object ball off of the cue ball into the pocket, rather than shooting the cue ball into the object ball. When I show this version of Reverse Billiards, many of the guys in the pool room think I'm teaching my students to scratch. In fact, what this does is give you a specific target to aim at off of the cue ball. You're now play-ing for a targeted area rather than all over the table, which helps you to play closer position when you go back to regular pool (Diagram 9). This game will help you get a more exact position with your cue ball, because it's helping you to focus more on the deflection angles.

In regular play, your cue ball is operating off of the object ball. All I've done here is to turn the situation around. By turning the natural order around, you can check your grasp of the skills. It's a form of cor-rection and will give you a different perspective, not only on these shots, but on the whole game. You'll become more familiar with the configurations and begin to pick out patterns.

At first, be sure to hit all these shots at medium speed. You'll want to pocket balls by hitting high, middle, and low. Pretty soon you'll find out that if you hit the ball a little slower you'll create one angle off of the cue ball and if you hit it harder you'll create another angle. A slow hit will lessen the angle, while a harder hit will widen the angle. You may also begin to see where you need to apply a little English. Because you're shooting the object ball off of the cue ball, you'll begin to realize that you can play position on the cue ball itself. By playing to bring the cue ball near the pocket, you'll start giving yourself easier shots. You'll begin playing position in the game, the cornerstone to accomplished play.

The beauty of reverse billiards is that it will give you a target. You're shooting the object ball at the cue ball and caroming it into the pocket. You can change the angle simply by hitting high, middle, low, or draw. Since the pocket is at least four and seven-eighths inches wide (side pockets are a little wider, up to five and three-eighths inches), you're working on positioning your cue ball more exactly. By playing this game, you begin to manipulate the position of the cue ball as well, which means you're starting to change the contact point. You can even learn to cheat the pocket. Though you know the ball will fit if you aim for the center of the pocket, you'll also learn that the angle of the carom allows you to shoot the ball in either of the sides of the pocket as well. By taking the size of the pocket into account, you can change the angle of deflection of the object ball off of the cue ball.

The difference between this method and English is that English forces you not only to change the contact point to pocket the object ball, but to take speed into consideration as well. The English will have more effect if you hit the ball with less force. Hitting the ball very hard all but neutralizes the English. It just complicates your shot and forces you to take more into consideration. If, instead, you can go with a center-ball hit, your chance of pocketing the shot improves tremendously.

I like to gauge my shots by looking to see whether I can use high, middle, low, or draw. If none of those options appear feasible, I begin to think about hitting the cue ball right or left of center. After so many years, I actually see lines all over the table every time I have to make a shot. Over time, you develop an almost innate response to situations, and a feel for how to hit. Play enough caroms, and your arsenal of strokes will increase dramatically.

In my classes, I teach my students to aim with their cue sticks. Of course, the reality is that you're aiming at the center of the cue ball, since you always want to think about skewering that ball with your stick. Even if you are aiming at a fraction on the object ball, you want to be sure that the cue travels right through the center of the cue ball in a straight line. Ultimately, you'll do wonders for your stroke, as well as your cue ball positioning and object ball pocketing.

Checklist

1. The base formula: strike the center of the cue ball with medium speed, and keep your cue stick level to get an 80 to 85-degree angle of deflection off the object ball.
2. When manipulating the angle of deflection by hitting above or below center-cue ball, raise or lower the bridge hand rather than elevating the butt of the cue stick.
3. If you choose a slower speed, or hit the cue ball higher, you lessen the angle of deflection.
4. If you choose a faster speed, or hit the cue ball below center with a flat stroke, you widen the angle of deflection.
5. Create draw by loosening your back hand and striking the cue ball at least two tips below center. Slightly elevate the back of your cue stick, and shoot straight through the area where your cue ball is located. Use a striped ball as a substitute for the cue ball to help you visualize the response of the cue ball.

ENGLISH

English just means striking the ball left or right of center. Its two functions—stopping or slowing down the movement or motoring around the table—are often misunderstood. A change in aim must take place as well.

Recreational players like to sound savvy by throwing the word "English" around—they approach it as a cure-all for any shot that looks difficult. Actually, putting spin on a ball (which is what English is) makes pocketing the object ball *more* difficult. Not only do you have to account for the curve in the cue ball's path and readjust your aim, but you have to select the accurate speed. With very few exceptions (which I discuss below), English should be used to position the cue ball rather than as a reliable pocketing technique.

One note before I go on. Chalking up properly is the sign of a good pool player—you should always be sure to do so for each shot. Applying English depends on adequate chalk. It was in Bartley's Billiard Room in Upper Bath that staffer Jack Carr realized that hitting the cue ball in different ways made it behave strangely. He could make it stop, back up, and curve. Carr called it side, but we call it English.

When you apply English to a cue ball it will curve in the same direction as the spin you put on it. If, for example, you put left English on the cue ball, the cue will force it off to the right, but the spin you have created by hitting the left side of the ball will cause it to curve back in that direction as it moves down the table (Diagram 10). The grade of that curve depends entirely on how far to the side the cue ball is struck, and the speed of your stroke. A slow hit will broaden the curve, a hard hit shortens it. In this way, English affects the path of the cue

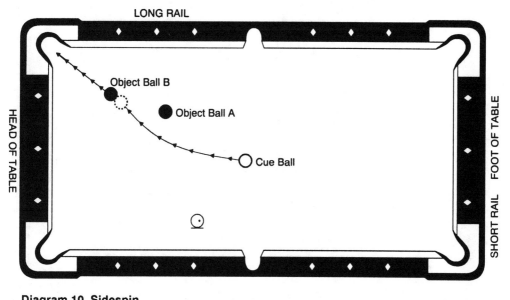

Diagram 10, Sidespin

Ball A lies between the cue ball and object ball B, obstructing the shot. By putting spin on the cue ball, we get past A and curve around for the hit on B.

ball on its way to the object ball, and its subsequent deflection off the rail (Diagram 11). Naturally, it also affects the path of the struck object ball. With right hand English you can expect the object ball to throw to the left, and vice versa. (See Chapter 3 for a discussion of throw.)

The greatest application of English you'll ever need is the distance of one cue tip right or left of center. You risk miscuing if you put too much English on the ball. One cue tip is the maximum, but this shouldn't keep you from experimenting with smaller contact areas. Try shooting at one quarter, one half, and three quarters of a cue tip of English (Diagram 11). With less spin, pocketing becomes easier because there's not as much of a curve on the cue ball to account for. Still, it can make all the difference when the cue ball makes contact with the rail.

Sailors have port and starboard, pool players talk about reverse and running and English rather than left or right (Diagram 12). Calling it right or left will only confuse you, since the direction of the English is determined by the angle of the shot. One way I keep them straight is to think of the high and low sides of the angle formed by your cue ball,

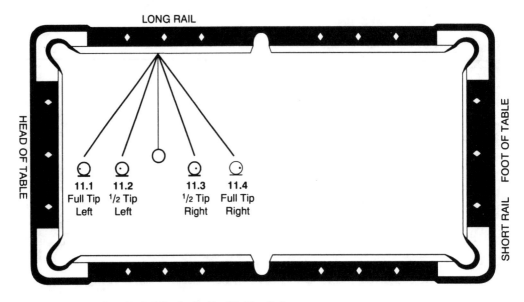

LONG RAIL

HEAD OF TABLE

FOOT OF TABLE

SHORT RAIL

11.1
Full Tip
Left

11.2
1/2 Tip
Left

11.3
1/2 Tip
Right

11.4
Full Tip
Right

Diagram 11, Cue Ball Off of a Rail with English
These angles assume that the cue ball is being hit straight into the rail at a medium speed. A harder-hit ball will have less of an angle, while a slowly hit ball's angle will be greater.

the pocket and the object ball. The object ball sits at the high side of the triangle; the base of the triangle is the low side.

Generally, the cue ball is traveling toward the high side of the angle, away from the low side. Reverse English is the low side of the angle, running English the high side. Think of running English widening the angle of the cue ball off the rail and thus increasing the cue ball's speed. Reverse English will shorten the angle and slow down the speed.

Not only are there two kinds of English, but there are also two ways to apply it to the ball: parallel and swivel. When you use the parallel method, you aim the stick at the center of the ball and then move your bridge hand to the left or the right while keeping the stick *absolutely* level. Be sure that both hands and your entire stick shift, not just the butt of the stick.

When you swivel, your bridge hand stays planted at center ball, but you move the butt of the cue stick to the right or left. You're actually shifting the nose of the cue stick as you keep your bridge rock steady. Swivelling will give you a little more spin, paralleling a little less. By using the swivel technique, you'll avoid moving more than a cue tip

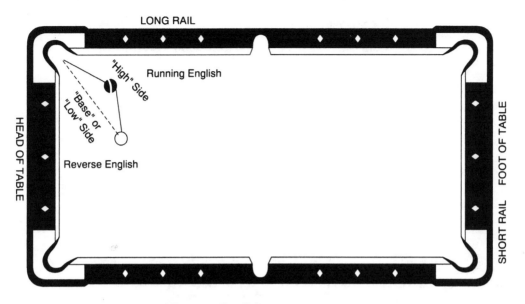

Diagram 12, Running and Reverse English

Running English is always on the high side, or apex, of the triangle. Reverse English is on the low side, or base. Reverse English serves to slow the cue ball down as it comes off of the object ball. Running English, as the name implies, will cause the cue ball to "run" faster, and thus move farther around the table.

from the center of the cue ball and, because you have more control over the cue, you will sidestep the danger of miscuing.

To understand how the cue ball curves with English, try to imagine a long shot with slow speed. The curve will be close to the cue ball's original position. As you increase the speed, the curve moves closer and closer to where the object ball is, because a faster-moving ball has less time to complete the curve. A ball that is spinning quickly also gets less traction on the cloth, which lessens the curve. For example, if you hit the ball harder in order to get it to travel a distance, the cue ball will curve closer to where the object ball is (Diagram 13). Be sure to take the speed into account when you aim at your object ball. The slower you hit the cue ball, the more curve the cue ball will have. If you put running English on a shot at slow speed, you'll have to hit the object ball more fully than if you use a medium speed, because the medium-speed shot will not throw the ball as drastically. Hitting the cue ball hard will effectively diminish any English you've applied to almost nothing by the time the cue ball makes contact with the object

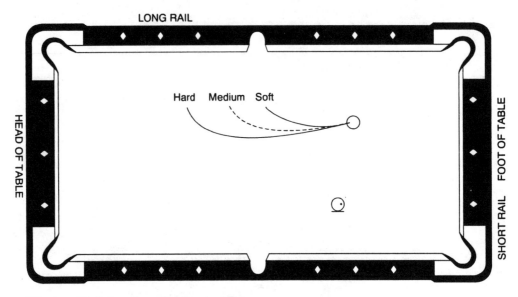

Diagram 13, Using Speed to Control Curve
The harder the cue ball is hit, the farther it will travel before it curves. This happens because a faster-moving ball does not grip the cloth of the table as readily as a slower one, so the spin takes longer to have an effect.

ball. Consequently, you don't have to change your aim very much with a hard hit on the cue ball. Sometimes not at all.

Remember, however, that the spin still affects the angle at which the cue ball comes off of the rail. Thus, if you prefer not to have to account for the effect of the cue ball's spin on the object ball, but still want to distort the cue ball's angle as it comes off of the rail, you can simply hit the cue ball harder. This will help you play position, and can also make your Straight Pool break more formidable. Object balls will spin in the opposite direction of the spin you apply to the cue ball, and you can use that increased action to loosen up the rack.

Keep your stroke in mind when you use English. You can apply the same amount of English using different stroking styles and see dramatic differences in the effect on the cue ball. Again, using a striped ball in place of the cue ball will help you see how subtle differences in stroke can affect the object ball. Hitting the cue ball low, or elevating the butt of the stick will exaggerate the curve of the cue ball. A masse shot is an extreme example of this sort of effect.

English is all about opposites. The effect of putting one kind of spin

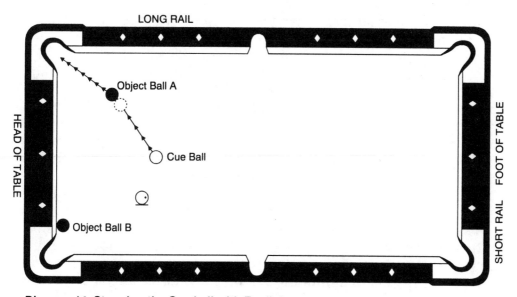

Diagram 14, Stopping the Cue ball with English

In order to get position on object ball B while pocketing A, you wish to stop the cue ball. Normally, this would not be possible, because of the angle of the shot. However, by using right-hand English on the cue ball, you are able to get a fuller hit on the object ball, since the spin will throw it left as it travels toward the pocket. If you hit the shot slowly, object ball A will curve into the pocket, and the cue ball will stay more or less in place.

on the cue ball will cause the object ball to spin in the opposite direction. Similarly, the technique itself can serve two apparently contradictory purposes. It can be used to slow down or stop the cue ball, as well as to motor it around the table.

Let's say you want to make your cue ball stop or come close to a complete stop. If you have a slight angle on the cue ball, applying English will enable you to have a fuller hit on the object ball. You might also think about hitting the cue ball a little low to increase spin (Diagram 14). If the angle on the shot is wide, the most you can do is to slow the cue ball down. (Many players unfamiliar with English believe that it can always stop a ball. Don't count on it unless your angle is fairly narrow.) The only sure way to stop the cue ball is to hit more mass on the object ball.

One way to visualize this is to think of a car heading for a brick wall. If it goes straight into the wall, the car will crumple to a complete stop. But, if the driver swerves sharply the car will deflect off the wall and continue. You're essentially "going straight into the wall" here by apply-ing spin to throw the object ball into the pocket. With more mass, your cue ball has a fuller hit, and that stops it, or at least slows it down.

You can also use English to create a new carom line off of the object ball. You know that when the cue ball hits the object ball at medium speed with center ball it travels off at almost a right angle from the object ball. (See Chapter Five for a more detailed discussion.) Now that you know about applying English, you can change the contact point on the object ball, thus forming a new line off of all but very thin cut shots. This will allow you to get a different position on the cue ball.

Sometimes this will involve combining high or low with running or reverse English to position yourself correctly. This means you can really start to mix things up. Suppose you have an object ball sitting at the spot you want your cue ball to strike on the rail. You can hit the cue ball high, which will shorten the angle and put running English on it. When the cue ball hits the rail on the shorter angle, the English

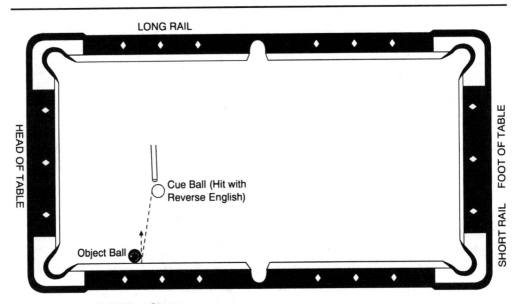

Diagram 15, Rail-First Shot

You have to use English to make this shot. Aim to hit the rail just in front of the object ball. Apply reverse English, that is, English on the same side of the pocket for which you are aiming. When the cue ball hits the rail, it will spin in the direction of the object ball, clip-ping the object ball as it comes off of the rail. The cue ball's spin imparts spin to the object ball, causing it to hug the rail. Be sure to execute this shot with a long, smooth, medium-speed stroke.

widens the angle of the cue ball. If you hit the ball lower (widening the angle) and add reverse English, you will shorten the angle when it hits the rail. After a while you'll begin to see that you're combining not only left and right, but also using different speeds and bringing high and low into play.

Pay special attention when you hit high or low with English, because the poles of the balls are smaller than the equator. Watch out for good stroke and follow through, because there's more danger of a miscue when you're aiming at a smaller area of the cue ball.

Earlier I mentioned that there are times when English can be useful to pocket balls. One instance is when a ball is frozen to a rail (Diagram 15). By using reverse (low side of the angle) you can hit the rail just before the object ball. This will cause the cue ball to spin in the direction of the object ball which makes it clip the object ball as it leaves the rail. There's now spin on the object ball, which will make it hug the rail—and drop right into the pocket—if you've done it right.

If a cue ball is shot straight into a rail using English, it will come off of the rail in the direction of the side of the ball to which spin was applied (Diagram 11). By experimenting with this, you'll master the technique of kicking a ball, which is very useful if another object ball is sitting against the rail at the spot your cue ball would ideally hit. To compensate for the difference in contact points, you have to use English to broaden or shorten the angle of the cue ball as it comes off of the rail.

Checklist

1. You do not usually need English to pocket an object ball, although there are a few shots with which it can help, or where it's even essential (Diagram 15).

2. Visualize a triangle between the cue ball, the object ball and the pocket. Running English is on the "high" side of the triangle and "reverse" English will move the cue ball toward the base side.

3. Use English to either stop your cue ball or limit its movement.

4. English can help you motor around the table or change the deflection of the cue ball off of the rail.

5. Speed of stroke will affect the amount of spin on both the cue ball and object balls. Slower speeds increase the amount of curve on both balls, while hard speeds minimize the effect until the cue ball hits the rail.

SEVEN

BANKING SYSTEMS

Two banking systems, the X-system and head and foot spot systems are explained. You will learn how to use the table as a guide for shooting.

Banking means hitting an object ball into a rail to pocket it on the opposite side. Learning to bank properly will help you to use the whole table. It will also help accustom you to seeing possibilities for difficult shots as you become familiar with the whole table.

Get to know the table you're using. All tables have their quirks, and you will want to test each of the six rails. If you warm up using the foot and head spots, you can check out all the rails to see that they are running true.

I am going to describe two banking systems. There are many systems, but these are the two I teach to beginners, and which I am most comfortable with. In both cases, you want to hit the center of the cue ball at medium speed—solidly, don't baby the ball. You'll develop a feel for when a harder hit is called for. When you hit the ball harder, it shortens the angle of deflection off the rail. Hitting the ball hard shortens the angle, because the object ball has less time to move over. It also compresses the ball into the rubber of the rail, which lessens the angle of the ball's rebound by snapping back into place with more force. If you hit the ball slowly, it compresses the rail less and has more time to widen its angle (Diagram 16).

X Marks the Spot

The first system I'm going to talk about is the X-system. Basically, it involves bisecting the angle made by the path of the object ball (Dia-

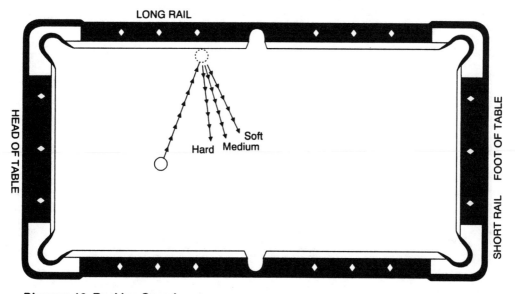

Diagram 16, Banking Speed

A harder-hit ball will come off of the rail at less of an angle than one hit at a slow speed. There are two reasons for this. First, the harder-hit ball has less time to move over after it comes off of the rail. Second, the rubber of the rail contracts more when hit hard, and thus snaps back harder, throwing the ball out at less of an angle.

gram 17). It makes no difference where your object ball is, but this system works best if your cue ball doesn't cross the line of the object ball as the object ball comes off the rail. Just to whet your appetite for the possibilities of banking, I will let you know that spin can add yet another dimension. If your cue ball is above or below the object ball, so that you have to cross the path of the object ball as it comes off the rail (Diagram 18.1), you'll have to account for this by applying English to the cue ball. If that sounds confusing, remember that when the cue ball crosses the object ball, you get spin. By putting English on the cue ball, you will counteract the effect. For the moment, though, stick with shots that do not require English.

Often, people get confused about how to widen or shorten the angle of an object ball off of the rail with English for banks (Diagram 18.2). Say you've got an object ball between the cue ball and the rail, and your pocket is to the right of the ball. You need to widen the object ball's path. If there were no cue ball to cope with, you would hit the

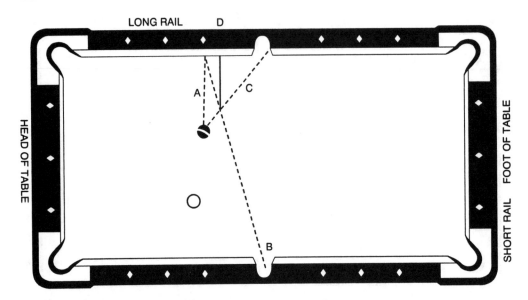

Diagram 17, X-System Banking

In this example, the ball is being banked across-side. Draw a line from the object ball to the rail (A). Then draw a line from that spot on the rail to the widest part of the pocket you're banking into (B). Draw another line from the object ball to the widest part of the pocket you're going into (C). There is an X where the two lines to the pocket meet. Drop another line to the rail at the meeting point of the X (D). Aim the object ball to hit the rail at point D in order to bank it. Use a firm, medium-speed stroke. The cue ball should be at an angle that will not cause it to cross the object ball's path as the object ball comes off of the rail.

object ball with right spin to widen the angle. This means you have to put left spin on your cue ball.

Again, this system assumes that you hit the cue ball dead-center at medium speed. You may hit the cue ball high, middle, or low, but not left or right of center. Remember the difference between low and draw. If you want the cue ball to draw, you need to hit it harder than when you want to slow it down. Hitting with a lot of draw lessens the angle of the object ball off of the rail a bit, because of the harder hit required to get draw on the cue ball.

Disregard the cue ball in making the X. To plot the X, you need to consider only the object ball, the pocket you want to sink it in and the opposite pocket.

From the object ball, draw a line straight into the rail that you plan

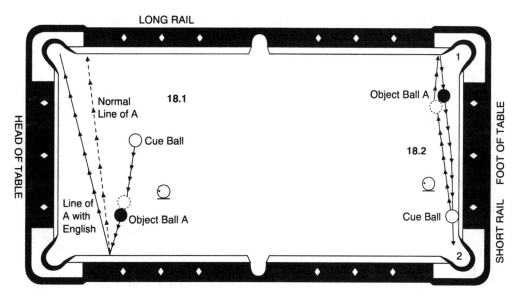

Diagram 18, English For Banks

18.1 Normally, this shot would not work with a straight hit on object ball A, because the natural angle will bring A up short of the pocket. However, by putting left (running) English on the cue ball, you impart right spin to A, which widens the angle and sends it into the pocket.

18.2 The cue ball is below object ball A, thus making a cut into pocket 1 impossible. By using left English on the cue ball, however, you impart right English to object ball A. This English causes A to shift right as it comes off of the rail, thus dropping it into pocket 2.

to bank from. (When you first try this, use cues to mark the lines. They will help you visualize these lines when you set up a shot in play.) Draw a line from that point on the rail to the pocket you plan to sink the ball into. Now go to the opposite pocket, and draw a line from the widest part of the pocket to the object ball. (Widest here means more than just the middle of the pocket. You want to find the area of the pocket that will give the greatest possibility of sinking the ball.) I must emphasize that you use the widest part of the pocket, especially on the side pockets. Depending upon the angle of the shot, the widest part of the pocket may not be the center of the pocket. The point at which the two lines converge is the X. (Your cues will actually cross here.) Now, imagine a perpendicular line from the X—where the two lines meet—into the rail. That is the point where you want to shoot the object ball into the rail.

The X-system is quite common, and pretty well-known. Unfortunately, it's been criticized by experts who insist you have to develop an eye for bank shots. I can't quibble with that, but I don't know a better way *to* develop an eye for banks than using this system. It's imperative that you develop a sense of the table. By taking the X-system and disciplining yourself to make those lines, mapping out the table will become second nature to you. Even after you start making the X in your head rather than laying out the cues, you'll find you use it again and again.

When the object ball is one to three inches from the rail, you can easily make the X in your head. Just be sure to cut the ball enough. This mistake is much like confusing "point of contact" with "point of aim" (see Chapter 4 for explanation). Be aware, however, that the X system does not work if the object ball is frozen to or within a half inch of the rail. In this case, the cue ball will interfere with the shot. So you'll have to use English to bank the ball, and to get the cue ball out of the way.

When I started playing, I used the X-system to figure out bank shots. I made sure that I kept using it, and finally reached the point where I could see the bisection without having to make the X. But even now, if I really need to make a bank shot—let's say it's match point—and I have any doubts, I always take a few seconds to make the X. I know the system is trustworthy, and by checking out the shot I get that extra little bit of confidence, so that I know exactly where on that rail I want to hit that ball. And confidence is key to this game.

Head and Foot Spots

Begin by looking at the table. There are two spots, the head and the foot. The foot spot is at the end of the table where the ball return is and where you rack up. The head spot is at the top of the table where the name plate is. (Some room owners skimp on the head spot, claiming that it's not important, but it's crucial to setting up shots.) Both the head and foot spots line up vertically in the center of the table at the middle diamond on the short rail. The head spot is lined up horizontally at the second diamond on the long rail down from the top corner pockets, the foot spot at the second diamond up from the lower corners. These are navigational tools, points of reference for various shots you make on the table, but especially for banking shots. There are connecting lines all over the table. The diamonds along the rails

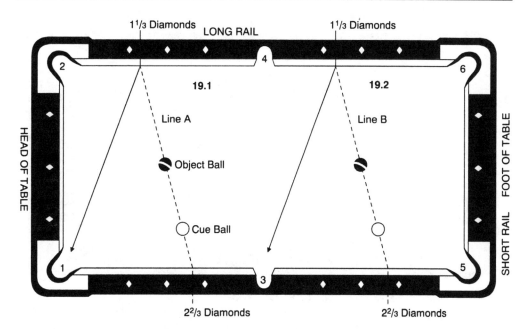

Diagram 19, Head- and Foot-spot Cross-table Banks

19.1 With the object ball sitting on the foot spot make the bank by hitting the object ball so that it contacts the rail one-and-one-third diamonds down from pocket 2. To better visualize this line, lay your cue stick down so that the tip is at the spot your object ball will make contact with the rail, and the butt is two-and-two-thirds diamonds down from pocket 1. In the diagram, the cue ball is sitting on this line (Line A), but this is not necessary to make the shot.

19.2 This is essentially the same shot, except that you are placing the object ball on the head spot and banking it into a side pocket. In this.case, the contact point for the object ball on the rail is one-and-one-third diamonds down from pocket 4. Similarly, line B runs between that point and two-and-two-thirds down from pocket 3. Again, the cue ball does not have to be on this line, it must simply cause the object ball to follow line B.

(the mother-of-pearl or plastic dots along the rails) can be connected to one another through mathematical formulas. These formulas are the basis for the banking systems (Diagrams 19–20). The foot and head spots can be used in the same way. Keep in mind that the connecting lines run through the spots from one rail to the opposite rail at a corresponding point.

There are six diamonds on the long side of the table (Diagram 20). Number these diamonds, starting with the corner pocket into which the object ball is being shot as zero. Count the side pockets as number

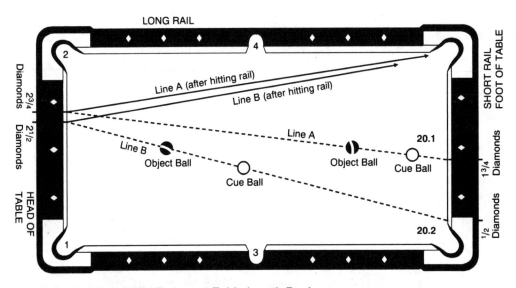

Diagram 20, Head- and Foot-spot Table-length Banks

20.1 The spots can also be used to make table-length banks. In both of these examples, you're banking into the upper right-hand corner pocket (pocket 6). Line A runs from the bottom rail at one-and-three-quarters diamonds above pocket 5, through the head spot to two-and-three-quarters diamonds above pocket 1. An object ball sitting anywhere on this line can be banked into pocket 6.

20.2 Line B runs from the bottom rail at one-half of a diamond from pocket 5, through the foot spot, to two-and-one-half diamonds above pocket 1. Again, a ball sitting anywhere along this line can be banked into pocket 6. As in diagram 19, the cue ball does not have to be sitting on the line. With both shots, you'll want to use a medium-hard stroke, since the object ball has to travel some distance to reach the pocket.

---

four and the opposite corner pockets as eight. Put an object ball on the foot spot and bank it across to the opposite corner (cross corner shot). Using the three diamonds along the lower part of the rail, find the two diamonds (on the opposite side of the table) that are closest to the pocket you're aiming at. Be sure to refer to the illustration. Assuming your cue ball is nearly straight on with, and behind the object ball, aim for one-third of the distance between the first and center diamond. Be sure to make your calculation all the way to the edge of the cushion. Naturally, you can also make this shot using the middle diamond and the diamond closest to the side pocket to bank the object ball across side.

You can use the X-system to double-check this theory. Place a ball on the spot and figure out a cross corner bank by making the X. It will work out to be one-third of the distance to the next diamond. Let's say you want to bank an object ball cross corner. Look for the connecting line through the foot or head spot to one-third of the distance to the first diamond on the rail that you plan to bank into from two-thirds of the distance to the middle diamond on the opposite rail. If the object ball lands anywhere along this line, you can bank the ball cross corner. The object ball does not have to be right on the spot, just along the connecting line. The process works for across side shots as well. Remember that the object ball must be on this line, but the cue ball can be off the line. As long as your cue ball doesn't cross the object ball, you can use the line as a guide.

I have been talking about going across the short side of the table, but you can also bank the object ball the length of the table. Let's say the object ball is on the foot spot, you're behind the ball, and you can't pocket the ball directly into the top corner or side. So you look for a way to bank it. Remember, you're aiming for the pocket opposite the point of contact with the rail. On this particular bank, you're going about one and three-quarters of the length of the table.

Look at the rail on the opposite end of the table (the foot), and you'll see only three diamonds. Look at the diamond closest to the pocket *opposite* the pocket you want to sink the ball into. If you're banking on the right side of the table, for example, it would be the top right hand pocket. Eyeball the distance between the middle and first diamond, but rather than dividing this into three parts, as you did when you shot across side, divide it into four. You'll need to hit the ball harder, because it's traveling nearly twice the length of the table. If you were to work out the X-system, you'd see that it actually bisects closer to one-third off the first diamond. But since you are hitting the ball harder for distance, you need to take the speed into account. You want the object ball to hit the rail one-quarter left of the first diamond towards the middle diamond. That is, one and one-fourth diamonds left of the right hand corner pocket. You may hit high, middle, or low, with medium-hard speed and a level cue stick.

Now let's say the cue ball is in the middle of the table, the object ball on the head spot and you are banking into the head rail to the lower pocket. You'll only have to travel one and a quarter of the table, which means that you don't have to hit hard. You can hit the ball (slightly harder) right between the first and middle diamond (closest to the pocket opposite of where you are looking to sink your ball). Because of the increase in speed, try to hit the rail just inside the halfway point in the direction of the first diamond.

Unfortunately, there is no substitute for play to get a feel for when to hit the ball hard and when to hit it slowly. You just have to spend lots of time to hone these skills.

The object ball can be in the center of the table and still on that continuous line. As I mentioned, the foot spot is the base of the line that runs the whole length of the table. (Naturally, the same system applies if your object ball is on the head spot.) Refer again to the diagram. The imaginary lines run from the bottom of the table, through their respective spots, and back up to the top of the table. You can put anything along this line and make the shot.

Eventually you'll begin to see the "lines" that cover the table, the first steps to kicking, banking, and playing position. Right now, become familiar with the spots as your guiding points. They're bases, especially for beginning players. The easiest lines to see are the ones through the foot and head spots—I often think there should be another spot directly halfway, which is the center of the table. If you become familiar with the head and foot spots as orienting points, the non-existent middle spot will start to help you as well.

DEFENSE, DEFENSE, DEFENSE

Defensive moves have often been characterized as "dirty pool." Explanations of legal defensive moves and strategies debunk this myth and show the excitement and challenge of playing defensively.

With the possible exception of bowling, or golf, every sport emphasizes some form of defensive strategy. One of the most exciting elements of pool playing is defense, and it takes no small skill to spot defensive maneuvers. But for years any defensive move in this game has been designated "dirty" pool. The problem is that pool rules can vary from venue to venue, and what's considered perfectly kosher in one hall can get you tarred and feathered in another. But since the Billiard Congress of America has codified the rules, there is no reason people shouldn't learn them. (Write to the Billiard Congress of America, 1901 Broadway, Suite 310, Iowa City, IA, 52240 for the official rules and record book. Or check at the desk of your local billiard parlor.) If both players are aware of the rules on legal shots and penalties, there is no reason not to include defensive play.

An important principle in defensive play is that you must always contact an object ball, after which either that ball, the cue ball or another object ball must hit a rail. Of course, if you pocket an object ball, you don't have to hit any rails. My definition of dirty pool is when someone just rolls a ball up to an object ball, without hitting any rails. Once everyone understands the rules and plays by them, defensive play becomes an integral and exciting part of the game. Don't eliminate it.

I have outlined the rules for the three standard games—8-Ball, 9-Ball and Straight Pool—along with the appropriate defensive strategies for each one.

8-Ball

This is the game most people know, in part because it's the one most often played on tavern tables. Rack the fifteen balls with the 8 in the center of the pyramid. The only requirement for racking is the 8 goes in the center, and a solid and a stripe in each corner. All the numbers above 8 are stripes, those below are solid. You may shoot at any ball until one is pocketed. That becomes the designated group for that player. (If you get one stripe and two solids, you're solids.) If you sink the 8 on the break at a pool hall table, it comes back up and doesn't

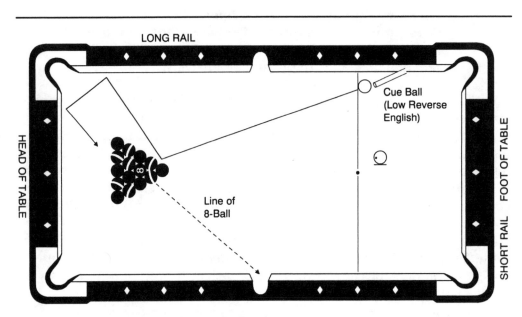

Diagram 21, Sinking the 8-Ball on the Break

Use a V-bridge on the rail. Place the cue ball about two balls' lengths to the right of the first diamond, just behind the headstring (left-handed shooters should execute this break from the left side of the table.) Strike the cue ball with two tips of low-reverse English (in this case, low left). Contact the second ball down from the pack as full-on as possible. The cue ball will break open the rack and go two rails to insure a second hit on any balls that might still be clustered in the rack area. The 8-ball will usually go into the left-side pocket.

count for or against you; if you make it on a coin-operated table, you win (Diagram 21). But if you pocket the 8, or make it jump off the table before the end of the game, it's a loss.

Although you don't have to call any other shots in the game, the 8 must be called. If you miss the 8 or make no contact with a rail, you don't lose, but your opponent gets cue ball in hand. A pocket scratch when sinking the 8 (the cueball is pocketed or you send the 8-ball into other than the designated pocket) loses the game. There's one more aspect to this rule that most players don't know about. A player who scratches while shooting at the 8-ball doesn't lose unless *both* the 8 and cue balls sink. In other words, if only the cue ball drops, the game continues, with the opposing player getting ball-in-hand.

In this game, balls need not go in clean. That means if you're shooting stripes and it caroms off a solid, it's okay. You may use your opponent's object balls to pocket your own, as long as you contact your own ball first. In this game, you can even miss the pocket you were aiming for, and the ball is still good if it goes in. For example, if you're shooting at a side pocket and the ball misses that pocket, hits the rail and falls into a pocket on the opposite side of the table, it still counts.

I get very upset when players try to claim that pocketed balls don't count if they make contact with an opponent's object balls. It's like hitting the backboard or the rim in basketball. It still counts as a dunk.

One mistake beginning players make in this game is to try to get rid of all their balls at once. A good way to think about this is to imagine the seven balls in your group as seven offensive and defensive players, a basketball team, just to stay with that analogy above. Let's say every time a member makes a basket, they have to leave the court. If you make six baskets, but your opponent has seven players on the field and you have just one, who do you think stands a better chance of winning the game? Pocketing balls can be as dangerous as removing a defensive player. Unless you can see your way clear to a sure run-out, don't pocket all your balls at once.

As a national 8-Ball champion, I won most of my games because I played defensively. While my opponent was busy plunking balls as fast as she could, I'd still have four or five balls on the table and suddenly I was the favorite. Using my remaining object balls defensively, I could snooker her or hide her behind one of my balls, and I kept getting cue ball in hand, because she was making fouls (Diagram 22). Finally, when I felt that I had a run in front of me, I would run through the balls.

How can you use the balls on the table? One tactic is to use the balls to block pockets and give your opponent fewer options for sinking balls.

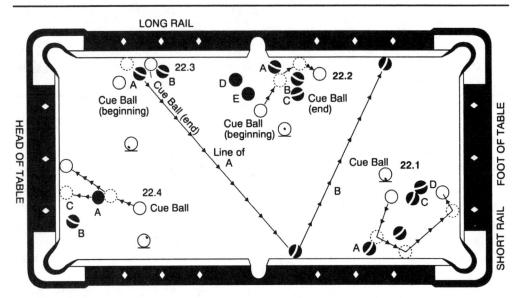

Diagram 22, 8-Ball Safeties

Sometimes, as the saying goes, the best offense is a good defense. If you can keep your opponent from making a shot, you can hold him off until he leaves you within a good position to run out.

22.1 By simply hitting the cue ball low, you bring it to the top of the table off of A and behind object balls C and D. Use a medium-speed hit. Keep in mind, as in Chapter Five, that sidespin is not necessary to bring the safety off, and in fact increases your chances of moving the cue ball too far.

22.2 Object balls A, B and C are your stripes, D and E are your opponent's solids. By cutting A thinly with a slow center-ball hit, you put the cue ball off of the rail behind B and C.

22.3 This is one of my favorites. With no shot on A and B, your stripes, you can snooker your opponent, while at the same time getting A and B out of each other's way for your next shot. With low running English (in this example, left) drive the cue ball into the rail just behind object ball A. The cue ball will come off of the rail, knock A off of the opposite rail, and come to a stop wedged between B and the rail.

22.4 This takes a certain amount of finesse, but if each of you only have one ball left on the table, it will really cause your opponent some trouble. Hit the cue ball high, on the running side of A with a slow stroke. A will come down to the rail between the cue ball and object ball B.

This is a little difficult if you are a rank beginner, but try to start thinking about this kind of strategy. Also, think about leaving your opponent in a bad spot—tied up on a rail, or one ball alone at the top of the table. Either of these situations make it very difficult to play position, whereas when a ball is in the center of the table you have lots of options.

There are also situations in which you will look as though you're tied up, but which can work to your benefit. Let's say you're stripes, and two of your stripes are clustered around a solid. You can pocket one of the stripes, but the solid can't be pocketed at all. In fact, when you pocket the open striped ball you'll break up the other two. Keep these two alone until near the end of the game, and leave your opponent stranded. You don't want to open them up for your opponent.

Now, if one of your balls is tied up with the 8-ball, you don't want to open up that 8 until you absolutely have to. Since your opponent can't win the game if the 8 isn't freed up, you have little to worry about. Especially if they've been rash enough to pocket all their own object balls already.

If I have a ball in a cluster with no opportunity to break it up, I try to open up the cluster by playing a safety rather than shoot at balls that are open until I have no choice but to go after the impossible shot. I'll make an open defensive move, snooker my opponent, for example, rather than shoot the open balls.

A table foul on your opponent's part gives you cue ball in hand. This is always an advantage and will allow you to make defensive moves in addition to putting you in a better position to pocket balls. For example, if you have two balls next to each other and can hide the cue ball behind your own (Diagram 22.3) you know they'll have to kick, which means hitting the rail before the object ball, driving any ball into the rail after contact. You may force your opponent to table scratch.

Cue ball in hand can also get you out of a tight spot. If you've had trouble reaching a ball, you can get it in a better position, or even pocket it, by placing the cue ball in a strategic position. That's why you want to be sure to leave at least two of your group on the table as long as you can. If you have only one ball left, your opponent can intentionally or accidentally pocket your last ball. And that leaves them the possibility of snookering you on the 8-ball, which spells big trouble. If your opponent pockets their ball and yours at the same time, it's a legal shot—and it's still their turn. (Many recreational players are confused by this rule, so it's worth making sure that your opponent knows this before you start.) Just remember, pocketing all of your balls without a sure shot at the 8 is kamikaze 8-ball.

If early in the game the 8-ball comes to rest next to a pocket, consider knocking it away with the cue ball, even though you will give your opponent cue ball in hand. Chances are that at an early stage it's a good move. Even better, see if there's a way to move the 8 and block the pocket with one of your own object balls. That's a very good defensive move.

9-Ball

The game most television viewers are familiar with is 9-Ball. Using only nine balls, you don't have to call pockets or balls. You must hit the lowest numbered ball on the table first. Provided you make contact with the 1 on the break, anything that drops in counts in your favor. The game does not begin until you contact the 1.

Any legal shot that pockets the 9 wins. It can be on the break, it can be the last ball on the table, it can be sheer luck. If you don't manage to hit the lowest numbered ball on the table and a rail your opponent gets cue ball in hand anywhere on the table. The only time you get the cue ball behind the head string is if you scratch on the break.

Four balls must hit the rails on the break. You have to really bust up the balls, because even if you manage to contact the 1, but don't get four balls to contact the rails, it's a foul. Your opponent has the option of cue ball in hand behind the head string, or making you shoot again. Three consecutive fouls is loss of game.

The first shot after the break can be a pushout, as long as you announce that that's what you're doing. A "pushout" means that you can do anything you want with the cue ball, except a pocket scratch or jumping the cue ball off the table. The incoming player has the option to accept the table or turn it back over to the player who pushed. For instance, if the 9-ball is sitting in a pocket and you don't have a shot at the 1, there's no way to play position so that you can get the 9. You can either pocket the 9 or just move it away from the pocket. If the 9 is pocketed on a push, it comes up on the spot, or as close as possible.

A push will get you out of a few difficulties. You want to push to a very tough safety, or a very tough shot. Or you can push to a place where your opponent can pocket one ball, but has only a tough shot to follow. You can also tie up two balls with a push and create more problems for your opponent. Just be sure not to hide yourself behind a higher numbered object ball. When you push, your opponent has the option of making you shoot again, so be careful not to snooker yourself.

One of the best defensive moves I've ever seen was by Mike Sigel. The 1-ball was in the middle of the top rail, and the cue ball was in the very center of the table. He was straight on with the 1-ball and the whole table was open. A pushout was his only option, and he called it and pocketed the 4-ball. He then left the cue ball on nearly the same spot, setting up almost the same shot as before. Not realizing the strategy, Mike's opponent told him to go ahead and shoot again. Mike paused, turned to the crowd and said, "The situation finally came up." He them leaned over, sank the 3-ball in the other pocket and gave his opponent the cue ball. And a big headache.

His opponent couldn't play safe off the 1, the 2 was down, the 4 was on the spot and the 3 was right behind it. Mike had tied up two balls and left his opponent with no way to snooker him. It was one of the smartest moves I've ever seen on a push shot.

A good defensive move in 9-ball involves looking for ways to pocket balls that will leave your opponent in trouble even if you miss. You want to try to make your opponent "safe" behind another ball or harm-less to you. (If your opponent can't see the ball, it's safe.)

Many times (Diagram 23) when you pocket a ball and play position on another ball, you may see that you have a steep cut shot into the corner pocket at the top of the table and your next shot may be at the bottom of the table. This may look like a tough shot to you. You can try

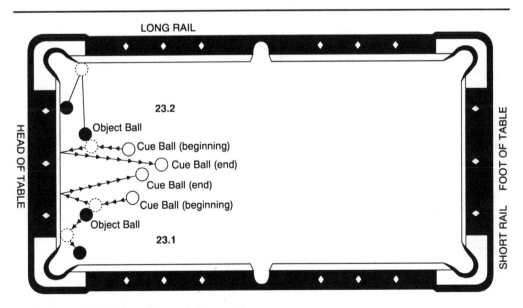

Diagram 23, Undercutting vs. Overcutting
By undercutting the object ball (23.1), you increase the odds of giving your opponent a shot if you miss. On the other hand, overcutting (23.2) will tend to leave a difficult bank or cut shot for your opponent should you not sink the ball.

to play position on the second ball, but you have to be careful of the speed at which you hit it. Also, if you cut a ball across the table, you'll see that if you undercut it, it will hit the top rail first and move out toward the center of the table. On the other hand, if you play the object ball that you're trying to pocket into the bottom of the pocket, you may undercut it if you miss. This will make it hit the side rail and float back toward the center, but again toward the top of the table. If you can learn to overcut you will leave your opponent with a bank or very tough shot rather than opening up the balls in the center of the table. Although this is an offensive tactic, its function is defensive.

Straight Pool

This is a call shot game. You rack up all fifteen balls. Two balls and the cue ball must hit the rail in the opening break. The incoming player can shoot at any ball on the table. The idea is to run the rack, and wherever the last ball and cue ball remain, they stay put. You then rack up the fourteen balls, and when you pocket that last open ball, ideally, you break up the rack at the same time and continue shooting until you miss or win.

Each ball earns a point. How many points you play to is up to you. Twenty-five is usually plenty for beginners, with fifty being an intermediate game. Pros in tournaments sometimes play to 200. If you don't touch any rails and you fail to pocket a ball, you scratch, but this will not give your opponent ball in hand. If you make three consecutive scratches (also called "fouls"), your opponent has two options. He can either take ball in hand, or make you take a penalty equal to 20% of the total number of points you are playing to. In other words, if you're playing to 100 points, the penalty is 20 balls. If you haven't sunk 20 balls, your score goes into negative numbers. Note that, if this latter option is chosen, the balls are reracked, and the player who made the fouls must break. If ball-in-hand is chosen, however, the balls stay where they are.

If the rack is closed, and your cue ball is in the center of the table—anywhere in a straight line up from the rack—and the top ball is missing (that is, you're trying to pocket the fifteenth ball) you may pocket the fifteenth ball but miss the rack completely. Now you're stuck in the middle of the table.

One possibility is to shoot your cue ball into the top two balls, favoring the inside of one of the top object balls. (If you're shooting into the

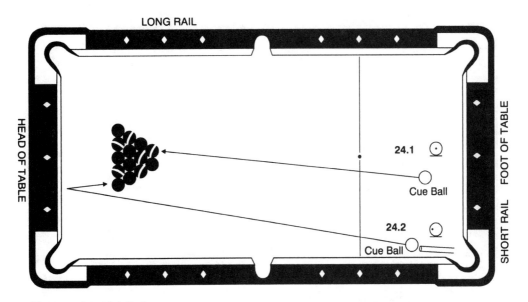

Diagram 24, 14.1 Defense

24.1 If the head ball is missing, and the cue ball is more or less straight above the pack, you can play safe off of either of the top two balls. Depending upon the angle of the cue ball in relation to those top two balls, contact the inside angle of the object ball with a center-ball, medium-speed hit on the cue ball. Elevate the cue stick slightly. One of the corner balls will hit the rail for a legal safety.

24.2 Even if the cue ball is too far to the side of the pack to play safe off of the top two balls, you can play a legal safety. Downstroke center-ball with a 45-degree elevation of the butt of your cue stick at medium-hard speed and one-half of a tip of reverse English (left in this example). Be sure to contact the rail directly below the corner ball, because the left-hand English will straighten the cue ball out. You want to contact the corner ball, freezing the cue ball there. One of the side balls in the rack will move out and hit the rail.

left side ball, you should favor the right side of the inside of the ball.) It's important that you hit the rack with enough speed that a corner ball comes out and hits the rail, ideally off the bottom rail and out into the table. That way you'll leave your opponent stuck on top of the rack (Diagram 24). When you play a safety off the rack in straight pool, you want to freeze your opponent at some point, but also bring a few of the object balls out into the open to make it difficult for your opponent to return the safety.

This applies to other pack shots as well. You might pocket the break ball and try to stop in an angle where you can play a safety off of one of

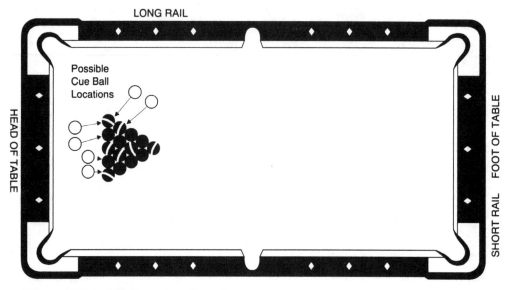

Diagram 25, 14.1 Defense (continued)
If the cue ball is below or to the side of the rack. play safe by wedging it between two object balls. In any of these cases, a corner or side ball will hit a rail, and the cue ball will stay frozen to the pack.

the two bottom balls in the rack (Diagram 25). You want to make sure you use just enough speed to send the corner ball to the bottom of the table, while leaving your opponent stuck in the side of the pack. Also, when you play this move, two balls come out. The ball on the opposite corner of the rack usually pops out and hits the rail on the other side of the table. Now you should have two open balls, one near the bottom rail and one near the long rail. This will leave your opponent with a difficult safety to play.

Remember that it's very tough when the stack has been disturbed to play safe off of the stack. Often I see players trying to skim the cue ball off of the rack and leave it right next to the rack. Even though they've played a legal safety, they've left their opponent near the stack. Thus the opponent can often turn the situation around by returning the safety. This just makes things easy for your opponent, because he has a selection of defensive moves he can play. Consider taking an intentional foul if you find yourself having to try to skim off of a loosened rack.

You can also call a safety, pocket a ball, and then that ball comes up on the foot spot, and your cue ball stays where it is. There's no penalty. Suppose your cue ball is on the top rail, along with the object ball and you're straight on which gives you no opportunity to break up the stack. You could call safe, pocket that ball, and bring the ball back up on to the table. When you're in the center of the table and the top ball is on the foot spot, the best safety is a two rail shot behind the stack, and your intention is to make a foul. You want to get the cue ball at the

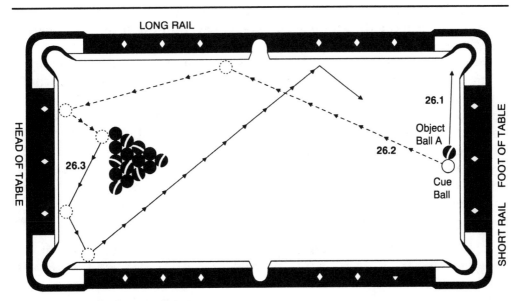

Diagram 26, 14.1 Safety Series

In Straight Pool, three consecutive fouls result in a 20 percent total penalty (in a game to 100 points, twenty balls), or ball in hand for the other player. Thus, if neither of you have a shot, but you can snooker your opponent into taking the first penalty, he will reach three fouls before you do.

26.1 Call a safety, and pocket object ball A in the corner. A comes back up and is placed on the head spot, at the top of the rack. Leave the cue ball in the center of the table, since that's the most difficult place from which to play a safety.

26.2 Your opponent should take an intentional foul by shooting along line A, which will take him two rails and into the back of the pack. If you're in this situation, downstroke the cue ball with a 30-to-45-degree angle on the cue stick at medium speed, center-ball. Try to knock a few object balls out of the rack with this shot, since that will make it more difficult for the opponent to leave you safe at the top of the table. If some balls come loose, the "safety battle" will take place behind the rack.

26.3 If no balls come loose from the pack return the intentional foul by shooting the cue ball two rails along line B and putting it at the top of the table.

back, but also knock a few object balls out. This will force your opponent to play safe, which will leave you near the balls rather than uptable and away from the balls (Diagram 26).

In most cases, you want to force your opponent to open up the balls for you. If it's a closed rack, be sure you can play off a ball to send your opponent back uptable. When the balls loosen up a little bit, even skimming a ball and going back uptable will usually open up a number of balls in the pack. If you put your opponent back uptable, and the rack is closed, they have nothing. They'll either have to take a second intentional foul, or they'll have to skim a ball and open up the rack for you. Most good players force their opponent to open up the balls.

To shoot or not to shoot? When exactly you take a shot is really a matter of feel and confidence. The hardest decision is between a difficult safety and a difficult shot.

I find the term "dirty pool" amusing, because to execute an effective safety requires imagination and creativity. Anyone who tells you not to play defensively doesn't understand the intricacies of the game. You have to think about the angle at which you'll contact the cue ball, the speed, and what stroke to use. The term "dirty pool" is just a misnomer for careful, skillful play that makes the game much more thrilling.

Some general thoughts on defense:

1. If your opponent is in stroke, and you're not quite up to snuff, try to break their momentum. Slow down a little, try to bait them with tough shots.

2. Snookering an opponent will usually take all the wind out of their sails. But remember that it works best in 8- or 9-Ball, since in Straight Pool they can make a legal shot off of any object ball on the table.

3. In order to work, defense has to be played just right.

4. Consider the percentages. Try to see what is likely to happen, rather than what you hope will happen. Defense means knowing the odds.

5. The worst mistake is not to take all of your options into account. Become familiar with all of the possibilities—speed, contact points and changing angles.

6. Most important: Once you decide on a shot, lean on it and shoot. If you're still wondering whether to do shot X or shot Y, stand up straight and think some more.

PRACTICE DRILLS AND PRACTICE GAMES

Practice drills to improve cueball positioning and pocketing are presented. Alternatives to the tedium of drills-only practice are also described.

Watch a great pool player run balls off a table, and you'll probably notice how easy they make it look. Even allowing for natural ability, the main secret is time. Every first-rate pool player has spent years getting their game together. Years of shooting, years of practice, years of trying to lead a normal life while they cater to their obsession. That's what makes them great players.

But even if your goals don't include the U.S. Open 9-Ball, there is nothing that will improve your game more than practice, practice, practice. You will become comfortable with your equipment, learn to control the balls, and acquire a feel for the game. The only way to shoot and shoot well is to make every movement second nature, to plan ahead, and to recognize what opportunities each of the patterns offer. And the only way to do this is to become as familiar with the table as with your own family: You have to feel completely at home there.

Because I know that practice and drills are not scintillating ways to pass the time, I've devised some games to sharpen your skills. The three games will help your game by isolating particular problems. Novices will find each one instructive, and more advanced players can use these games to highlight weaknesses and work on them.

Indirect

In this game, you may use any ruse to pocket the object balls—except to shoot them straight in. Use banking, caroming, kicking, or combination shots. The idea is to make things complicated for yourself.

Rack the balls in a full rack, just as you would for 14.1 Straight Pad. (The cue ball is used normally in this game.) Again, you must call your shots. The player who pockets eight points first wins the game.

All illegally pocketed or uncalled balls get spotted. If you do not pocket a ball, something must hit a rail. If you scratch, it is ball-in-hand to the incoming player, except on the break when it's "behind the line."

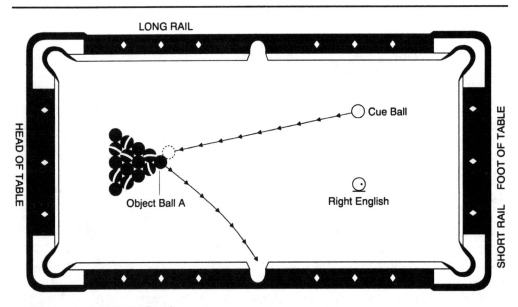

Diagram 27, Indirect Break

Put the cue ball one diamond out from the rail on the head string. In this scenario, the cue ball is on the right side of the rack, so use right English, and hit the head ball a little to the right. With practice—and a tight rack—you'll sink the head ball in the side pocket.

The only rule governing the opening break in Indirect is that, if you don't pocket a ball, any two balls, including the cue ball, must hit a rail. If the ball you pocketed was not "called" it comes up, and your turn is over.

Remember, every shot must be something other than straight in. A popular opening for Indirect is to bank one of the corner balls in the rack off of the bottom rail into an upper corner pocket (Diagram 27). It's a good shot to play, although it doesn't open the rack very much. My good friend Bob Worth showed me a creative way to pocket the head ball in the side pocket, opening the rack wide.

Put the cue ball along the line of the first diamond from the top rail, and bring it down even with the head string. Hit the head ball a little bit to the side, applying some English. If the cue ball is on the right, you hit the head ball a little to the right, putting a bit of right-hand English on the cue ball. Hit it at medium speed, and you might make that head ball fall into the left-side pocket. Since the head-ball will carom off of the two balls behind it in the rack, the shot is legal (Diagram 28).

Four Pockets

This is a fantastic game to teach cue ball control, and controlling the cue ball is the lifeblood of the game. Four Pockets also teaches you a great deal about pattern play.

Begin by setting aside the number of balls that you think you can run. You can start with as few as five, or get as ambitious as eleven. Experts use all fifteen. You get one point for each ball pocketed, and two chances to score bonus points.

If your last shot sends the cue ball through the rack area (the triangular area below the foot spot), you get five bonus points. If you run the balls straight through, you get one point for each ball (seven, in my example), plus five points for the run. Thus, your possible total is seventeen points.

If you do run all of your balls *and* send the cue ball through the rack area on the last shot, it's still your turn. Your opponent must place the seven balls back on the table, and you start off again with ball-in-hand. There is one important factor to note when taking the shot on the last ball. Since Four Pockets is intended primarily to improve your Straight Pool game, the cue ball must not pass through the rack area until *after* it hits the object ball. This is because, in a Straight Pool game, the balls are brought up and reracked when there is only one object ball (the "break" ball) left on the table. If the cue ball had to come through the rack area on the way to the break ball in a straight pool game, it would be blocked by the fourteen racked balls. Even though the balls aren't reracked in four pockets as in straight pool, the rule applies, and you must be able to hit the break ball without first passing through the rack area.

Scratching at any time during your turn loses you a point, and your turn ends.

Let's say you begin with seven balls. Spread them out on the bottom half of the table (from the side pocket down to the foot). Be sure to place at least three balls on the table as possible break shots, just like straight pool.

You may only shoot the object balls into the four bottom pockets, but your cue ball is allowed to travel anywhere on the table.

Begin by taking cue ball in hand. The cue ball may touch only the designated object ball, or it's a miss. Don't touch any other object balls. If you do, that counts as a miss and you do not get credit for any ball pocketed on that shot.

You may find it difficult to visualize the rack area. Try laying it on the foot spot to get a clear idea of the area, and then remember where you'll have to pass through. This will develop your imaginative capabilities, which are very important in mapping a table during a game.

As in other games, you must always hit the ball and a rail, or you lose a point.

If your last object ball is in the rack, you spot it on the head spot just like Straight Pool. As long as you don't use the two top pockets, you can still pocket the ball by banking it.

Players often come to me and say they love Straight Pool, but can only run ten balls, or even a rack, before they have trouble. Usually, their problem is the other object balls. They keep hitting them as they make their shots. My policy is, when you don't touch anything, you know where everything is.

Many times you'll inadvertently tie up another object ball by touching it, or you'll get it frozen to the rail where your options are limited.

Playing Four Pockets will teach you to control the cue ball so that it doesn't go flying. When you play Straight Pool and the balls are open, you'll start running the balls if you can keep from touching other balls. Once you touch them, you can guess where they might end up, but you don't really know. If you pick your way around them, everything stays in a nice pattern, ready for you to shoot when you can.

If you play Four Pockets, you will see lots of improvement in your ability to run balls. As your initial spread becomes easier, add another ball.

This is also a good game to play against better players, as long as they give you a handicap. When I play with my students, I use eleven balls, they have seven. In addition, I can only score seventeen points for any one rack just like them. Naturally, it's much easier to touch other object balls with eleven balls on the table. Watching me, my students can learn to see patterns, to move around the table, and how to use the center area to orient themselves on the table.

When you play Straight Pool, you have to think in terms of open areas, zoning off sections of the table. You want to clear areas of the table. Four Pockets will really help you to do this. When I sit on the

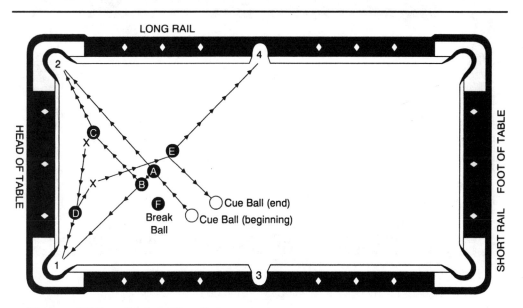

Diagram 28, Four Pockets Run-Out

1) Pocket object ball A in pocket 2. Stop cue ball.

2) Drop object ball B in pocket 1. Stop cue ball.

3) Pocket object ball C in 2. Leave cue ball just below object ball D.

4) Sink object ball D in pocket 1. Use draw to set up for object ball E with a slight angle.

5) Drop object ball E in pocket 4. Use draw to set up for the break shot on ball F.

sidelines, I see new players try to get out of the rack. Beginners will often choose the wrong ball, discovering their mistake a few shots later when they can't move anywhere. This game is great for teaching pattern play, controlling the cue ball and clearing zones on the table, and will really help your Straight Pool game. Not to mention that it will add variety to your shooting, and give you tangible goals as you add more object balls to the mix.

Roger Starr of the *New York Times*, a student of mine for years, always had problems with the last few balls before the break shot in Straight Pool. I noticed that much of his difficulty came from his cue ball bumping into other balls. He was either tying up object balls or putting them into tough pocketing positions on the table.

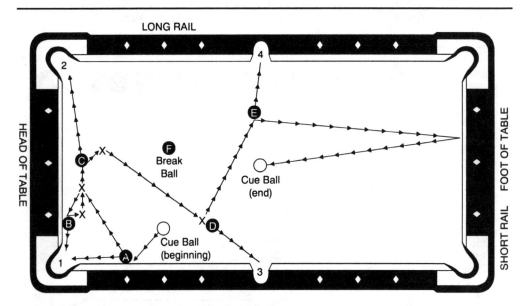

Diagram 29, Another Four Pockets Run-Out

1) Sink object ball A in pocket 1. Use topspin to set up for B.

2) Pocket object ball B in 1. Flat draw will bring you straight off of the rail. Leave a slight angle on C.

3) Drop object ball C in pocket 2. Flat draw will leave you with a slight angle on object ball D.

4) Pocket object ball D in pocket 3. Stop the cue ball for an angle on E.

5) Drop object ball E into pocket 4. Use flat draw to come off of the top rail back to the center of the table for the break shot.

I invented Four Pockets to increase Roger's knowledge of pattern play. Diagrams (28 and 29) show challenging layouts using six object balls. Remember, you're starting out with the cue ball in hand. If your cue ball touches an object ball other than the one you're pocketing it's considered a miss. And you can only use the four bottom pockets. Note that avoiding the rails is another key technique for successful position play.

Pep Talk

By now my system should be very clear to you. The basis of all my teaching is to hit the cue ball in the center, with a level cue stick at medium speed. If you use this idea as a starting point, you can get as fancy as you like. You'll always have a steady base.

I don't expect pool to play the role in your life that it does in mine, but I can't emphasize the benefits of practicing enough. No matter how naturally gifted you are, you've got to log in hours of playing to see improvements. My instruction rests on the idea that each technique will be practiced, practiced, practiced. That's why it helps to be obsessed.

But even if you only have a few hours a week, you will see dramatic improvements if you structure your practice and games to work on weak spots. By organizing your time, you will find your concentration improving as well. To play pool well, you've got to be able to shut every distraction out, not always easy with jukeboxes, conversations, and other players competing for your attention. Narrowing your focus to the table takes time to learn, but it's worth it.

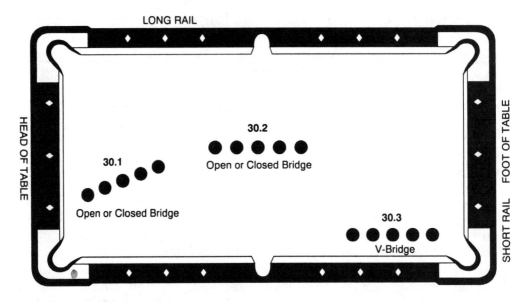

Diagram 30, Beginner Practice Drill

My former manager, Jackie Cooper, decided to take some pool lessons from me. Jackie had no hand-eye coordination at all. However, she was determined to learn just enough to enable her to become her husband's partner in a local 8-Ball league. I had to figure out a way to cure her of her fear of hitting the ball, and at the same time make her feel more comfortable with her stance, hand-bridges and back hand. If you share Jackie's problem, this drill is for you.

If holding the cue stick, pocketing or even making handbridges gives you trouble, this exercise will help. Pocket the object balls without using the cue ball. Use an open or closed bridge for 30.1 and 30.2. Use the V-bridge for 30.3. Pocket the object balls left to right, then from right to left. Concentrate on a rhythmic motion and steady speed. Practice each drill five times.

This will help you to feel more comfortable with your stance and bridges as you develop your eye.

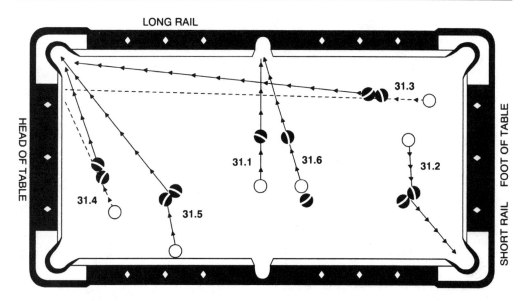

Diagram 31, Beginner Six Hand-Bridges

As Jackie Cooper became more comfortable with pocketing object balls without the cue ball, I slowly started her on drills which included the cue ball. It was important for the drill to focus on the six hand-bridges.

The simple, straight-in shots forced Jackie to keep her stick in a straight, level line, and to hit the ball at medium speed. This helped her to develop the stroke in her back hand. The caroms and throws were important for two reasons. She had to think about them when she set them up, which led her to recognize those types of combinations in game situations. Second, once you understand them, caroms and throws are simple shots to pocket. Therefore, Jackie was building her confidence in pocketing.

Set 31.1-.6 up, and shoot each five times. Use medium speed, and keep your cue stick as level as possible, especially on the rail bridges. Use the bridges as follows:

31.1—Closed Standard

31.2—Open

31.3—V-Bridge

31.4—Half-Bridge

31.5—Open Rail

31.6—Over-the-Ball

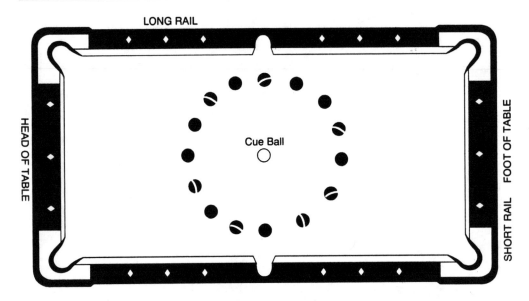

Diagram 32, Intermediate Practice Drill

The circle drill emphasizes two main themes; shot selection and "holding" the cue ball with English. In order to stay within the circle, you will have to choose shots which allow the cue ball to contact the mass of the object ball. This minimizes the movement of the cue ball. While doing the drill, notice that a back-and-forth pattern begins to emerge. If you shoot a ball into one of the lower corner pockets, your next shot will most likely be in a top corner pocket. The side-pocket shots are used to get you back in line with corner-for-corner pocket shots. When you end up with a slight angle on the object ball, use a small amount of English (no more than a tip) to spin the object ball into a pocket. Using spin means that you can contact more mass on the object ball, allowing you to contain the cue ball within the circle. You'll also need small amounts of draw.

This drill begins to develop what pool players call the "shot game." It will help you in all games, but especially in 14.1 and 8-Ball.

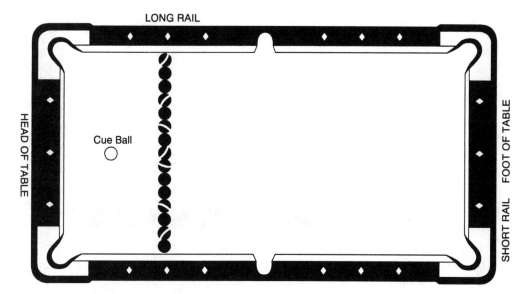

LONG RAIL

HEAD OF TABLE

Cue Ball

FOOT OF TABLE

SHORT RAIL

Diagram 33, Intermediate Practice Drill

Place fifteen object balls in a row along the foot spot line. Keep the cue ball in the space below the line, and try to pocket the balls in the top four pockets. If you get out of position, place the cue ball where you have a shot. If you miss an object ball, remove it from the table and keep going.

The "line up" drill emphasizes all of the skills described in the circle drill. Obviously, the main difference is that you can now use one or more rails to get position. Be sure to experiment with high, middle, low, and draw. Watch the angles of deflection of the cue ball off of the rail as you mix up where the stick contacts the cue ball. Keep your cue as level as possible, and, for the most part, use medium speed.

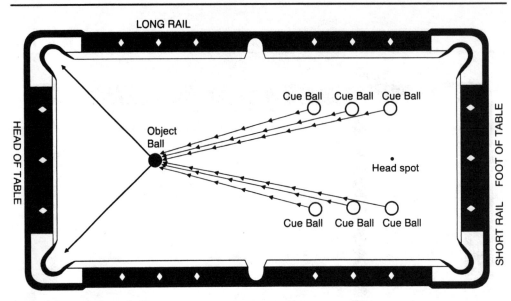

Diagram 34, Spot Drill

Place the object ball on the foot spot, and sink three in a row from each of the six cue ball positions shown.

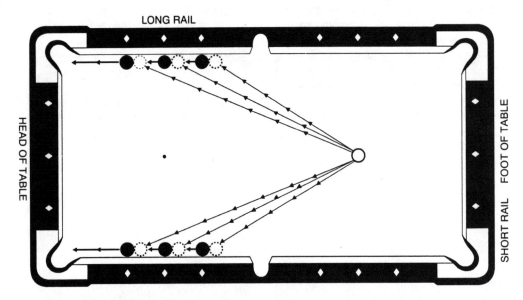

Diagram 35, Running the Rail

With the cue ball on the head spot, place the object ball against the rail at the first diamond. After three in a row here, go to the second diamond, and so on, until you've made the shot from all six diamonds.

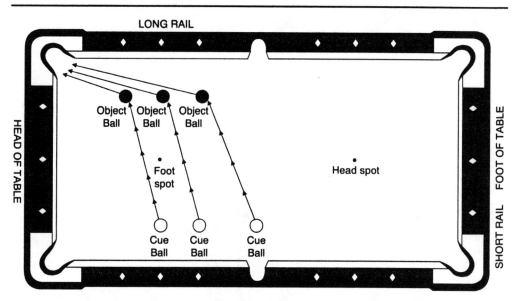

Diagram 36, Cutting Drill

Place the object ball at the point where the first diamonds of the short and long rails would cross. Put the cue ball at the same cross, one diamond down and across the table. Again, do three in a row from each diamond on either side of the table. This is a good drill to break in your Whizwheel on.

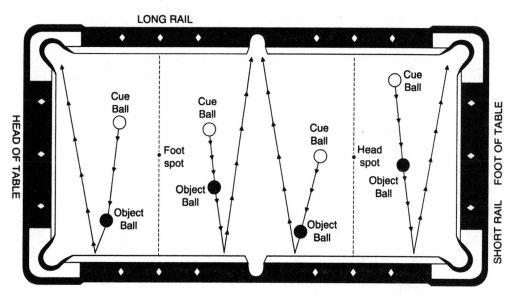

Diagram 37, Banks

Put your X- and spot-banking systems to use by shooting bank shots at random angles, three in a row into each pocket. Hit the side pocket twice; once from either side.

GLOSSARY AND POOL SLANG

Bank—shooting an object ball off of one or more rails into a pocket.

Billiards—the generic term for all types of pool and carom games. Specifically, games played on a pocketless table.

Break—the opening shot of the game. Striking the racked up object balls with the cue ball.

Bridge—the position of the hand on the table as it holds the cue stick.

Call shot—shot in which player announces specific ball to be pocketed in a designated pocket.

Cheat the pocket—playing the object ball into either the left or right side of the pocket to create an angle on the cue ball for positioning purposes.

Count—the score.

Cue ball in hand—license to put the cue ball anywhere.

Cushion—the ridge that runs along the rails.

Dead ball—when the cue ball comes to a complete stop upon contact with an object ball.

Double bank—intentionally shooting a ball off a rail into the opposite rail and back again into a pocket on the original rail.

Draw—stroking the cue ball low with a lot of follow-through causes it to boomerang off of an object ball.

English—spin put on cue ball.

Flat draw—low stroke that widens the angle or rebound of the cue ball off of the object ball.

Follow—stroking method that sends the cue ball in the same direction as the contacted object ball.

Follow through—moving the cue stick "through" the cue ball after actual contact with the cue ball.

Foot spot—point marked on the cloth two diamonds from the foot rail.

Foul—an infraction of the rules which terminates a player's turn at the table.

Frozen—balls that are touching each other on the table, or touching a cushion.

Getting shape—good position on the next ball after a shot.

Go in clean—the pocketed object ball sinks without touching another object ball.

Head spot—point two diamonds from the center of the head rail.

Inning—turn at the table.

Kick—shooting the cue ball into one or more rails in order to contact or pocket a specific object ball.

Kiss—a carom, either from the cue ball to several object balls or among object balls only.

Lagging—procedure for determining who shoots first. Each player places a ball behind the head string and banks it off of the fool rail. The player whose ball stops closest to the head rail can choose to shoot first or second. Note that contacting the back rail is legal.

Miscue—when tip of cue slides off of the cue ball because of inadequate chalking, a defective tip, or misapplied English.

Miss—any shot not completed successfully. May or may not be a foul, depending on the game.

Park your ball—the cue ball comes to a stop dead center in the table after a 9-ball break.

Pattern play—shooting the balls in a particular order.

Position—intentional placement of the cue ball after a shot.

Pushout—in 9-ball, the first shot after the break can be used as a "free shot." That means you can do anything you want with the cue ball—except commit a pocket scratch or jump the cue ball off of the table—without making a foul. The incoming player has the option to accept the table or turn it back over to the player who "pushed."

Rack—triangle used to pyramid balls at foot spot to begin a new game.

Ride the 9—taking a wild shot at the 9-ball, hoping to get lucky.

Run—series of consecutive scores in one inning.

Run out—shooting all the balls needed to win the game without a miss.

Safety—a defensive move in which the shooter hits an object ball into a rail to prevent opponent's shot.

Scratch—to sink the cue ball.

Sideboard or big pocket—when an object ball sits next to a pocket, guaranteeing that a ball shot into that pocket will go in on a carom, even if the player has a near miss.

Snooker—pocket game played on a 6 by 12 foot table with cue ball, fifteen red and seven colored object balls.

Spotting—returning the balls to the table as specified by the rules of the game.